Surviving Suicide

Help to Heal Your Heart

Surviving Suicide

Help to Heal Your Heart

Life Stories from Those Left Behind

by Heather Hays

Surviving Suicide

Help to Heal Your Heart

Life Stories from Those Left Behind

For information, please contact:
Brown Books Publishing Group
16200 North Dallas Parkway, Suite 170
Dallas, Texas 75248
www.brownbooks.com
972-381-0009
A New Era in Publishing™

Hardbound ISBN: 1-933285-29-X
LCCN 2005908952
1 2 3 4 5 6 7 8 9 10

Cover photograph by Twain Newhart/Hawaii

Biography photograph by Jeff Persichitte
www.friscophotography.com

Hair and makeup by Nicole Persichitte

To Brett, with Love

Contents

Contents

Contents

Acknowledgements

This book would never have become a reality without those who opened their hearts to me. People from around the world shared their tears and their triumphs. Their survival is the very soul of this book, and I can never show them enough gratitude.

My family has also been an incredible source of strength. I want to thank them for that, beginning with my father. He is an endless inspiration. As a forensic psychologist, he has seen a lot of pain, but he has also learned how people heal. He shares that in the section "Why Writing Heals." Dad, thank you for being part of this journey.

My mother taught me to be truly aware of my feelings; it's hard to do, but always well worth it. She lost one of her dear friends to suicide. You can read about her loss in "The War and the Wall." Mom, I will always cherish you.

To my brothers Chris and Will—being there for me when Brett left us meant more than I have ever said. I couldn't have made it without you. You both gave me courage when I had none.

To my brothers Seth and Josh—you two are here holding my hand, even though we are miles apart. You are on your own journeys now. Know that I am with you.

To my youngest brothers Troy and Pierce—the world holds so much for you. Embrace it all.

To my sister, Hollie, my right-hand woman, you were there for the long and sometimes tearful nights. You are my treasure.

Granny, you are the kind of woman I hope to be one day. Thank you for your guidance.

Karen, your advice always comes from the heart. John, your giving spirit is a guide, and I am glad you share it.

Nothing in the world is as valuable as a friend. I am blessed to have so many friends who share hugs and heart-to-heart talks. Julie, you are a part of me, and always will be. Shannon, you have a beautiful soul, and I am honored to call you my friend. Kim, much of my conviction to continue comes from you. Heidi, you are one of the truest people I know. Tena, I thank you for sharing your gift of song. Your voice and words are angelic. Amy, you always know the right thing to say to me. Thank you.

Karen, you pushed me when I needed it. Baron, you taught me to stop and smell the flowers. Jeff, thanks for letting me follow in your footsteps. Steve, you still listen and that means so much.

Evan, you are my mentor and my muse, as well as a constant source of entertainment and encouragement. Of course, without Becky, there would be no Evan. Becky, thank you for making it all possible.

To my friends in Hawaii—Amos, Carolyn, GeriAnn, Randy, Susan, Ann, Twain, Andre', Alan, Stuart, Colleen, Alton, Julie, Eric, Dave, Nancy, Mike, Pi'ilani, Joe, and those at Chaminade University—I love you all.

To my friends in Yakima and Green Bay—Mark, Kathy, Valerie, Susan, Ann, Tedd, Preston, JB, Randy, Judy, Dan, Marian, Lloyd, Joel, Reggie, Sara, Jason, Jay, Shelley, Kristine, Kevin, Tanya, Bonnie, Mr. T., the Good Neighbor Radio Show, the Yakima Police Department, KNDO, and WGBA—you were my rock and I thank you.

I could not have completed this journey without Christian, Belita, Ron, Kristin, Julie, Nicole, Kevin, Mary, Susan, Shelley, Jason, Marie-Clare, Christine, Tracy, Kim, and Jen. For helping me bring this journey to the next level, my heart goes to Jeff.

I also want to thank my FOX family in Dallas for encouraging me to share this story. Thank you, Kathy and Maria.

Acknowledgements

A huge thank-you belongs to Milli Brown, Kathryn Grant, Ted Ruybal, Deanne Dice, and the rest of the staff at Brown Books Publishing Group for helping me share this message of hope with a wider audience.

To Pastor Ed Young, Dr. Norman Giddan, Charlotte Dunhill, Linda Runnells, and Diane Weatherford—thank you for your incredible insight on healing one's heart.

And lastly, I want to thank a man who has been part of this book since the beginning. Wade, for your encouragement to explore my past, I will always be grateful, and I will always love you.

I am forever thankful to all of you for believing in me when I didn't believe in myself.

Introduction

Since you are reading this, you have probably lost someone close to you. Or perhaps you know someone who has lost a loved one to suicide. First, I want you to know how sorry I am for your loss. My heart breaks every time I hear of another person left behind.

I, too, am one of those people. My fiancé, Brett, woke up one October morning, showered, dressed for work, and went into the garage. After locking the door behind him, he started his vehicle and closed his eyes forever.

No matter how your loved one leaves your life, there are feelings of isolation and grief, anger and guilt. But suicide is one of the most painful ways to lose a loved one. It is chaotic and confusing—feelings that can often be calmed with answers and understanding—but with suicide, you rarely find either. I hope you can find comfort in reading the words from those left behind, as well as counselors and clergy who offer everyday ways to heal your heart.

Gathering life stories for this book was part of my own healing process. The stories are about people from all over the world—fathers and mothers, sisters and brothers, friends and lovers—all who ended their lives. The letters that follow the stories are written by their loved ones who were left behind.

The letters explore where we are during different stages of healing. One is from a four-year-old who lost her father when he took his life in their backyard. Another is from a woman in her sixties whose sister suicided twenty years ago. Read the words she wrote to her sister then and the ones she writes now.

You will also read the life stories of others caught in the complexity of grief: a woman agonizes over the suicides of her mother, husband, and son; a sister still has nightmares after seeing her brother shoot himself; a man shares the last words his sister wrote after she decided not to let cancer win; a woman watches her sister fight postpartum depression, and lose; and a teen still feels her dying lover in her arms. Tragic stories, yes, but each person in this book wants to share them. They want you to know you are not alone. Their e-mail addresses are listed in the back of the book so you can write them and continue sharing stories to help heal hearts.

I remember cleaning out a closet years after Brett's death and finding a letter I had written to him right after I spread his ashes in Hawaii. I sat on the floor and read that letter over and over again. I felt so alone when I wrote it and even more alone reading it all that time later. I don't want anyone else to feel that emptiness. That's why I gathered these stories.

Brett's spirit will live on through this book. I thank him for giving me the courage to write it. And I thank you for having the courage to take care of yourself.

Foreword

Every forty seconds, someone suicides. The World Health Organization also estimates that about one million suicide deaths occur each year. Suicide does not discriminate, and it knows no boundaries. As a therapist, I treat both suicidal adults and adolescents and have seen suicide deliver a profound sense of contagious sadness. I have also experienced that sadness personally.

My heart broke for a longtime friend when she called, crying, saying she had found a friend of ours unconscious on the bathroom floor. She said Carol had overdosed on prescription medication. She got there in time to save Carol, who insisted it was an accident. A few months later, I found out it truly was no accident. It was my turn to find Carol, and that time she did not survive.

I know Carol was not thinking about the consequences her death would have on me or anyone else. A person who suicides is typically not in a place to rationally understand what his or her death will do to those left behind. The rest of us just have to pick up the pieces.

As a survivor, and as someone who works with survivors, I have felt and seen the broad range of emotions that comes with being left behind: denial, anger, resentment, blame, guilt, shock, helplessness, and confusion. You must acknowledge those feelings and accept them. Acceptance is where the healing process begins.

Suicide often seems preventable, which can increase feelings of guilt and anger. Perhaps the person gave some indication of suicidal intent, and maybe those intentions went unnoticed until too late. You may then find yourself questioning your own actions. Did I ignore his pleas? Did I not see the signs? So many questions arise during the healing process, and there are so few answers. You want to understand how the suicide could have happened. You have to accept that you probably never will.

I have seen family members and loved ones turn against one another in an attempt to answer, "Why?" Often they blame someone for the circumstances leading to the suicide. I have also seen those outside the family cast blame. They sometimes look at loved ones as responsible, at least to some extent. Because suicide is self-inflicted, people often feel a need to assign blame as a means of making sense out of a senseless tragedy. If you understand that blame is born out of that need, perhaps you can let it go.

Healing is complicated and painful. It takes time, and quick fixes will probably not be effective in the long run. Talking, therapy, exercise, proper nutrition, support groups, and possibly medication can all help ease symptoms of depression. Although resources exist to help you, no one can take away your pain entirely. A conscious decision must be made to do the work necessary for your recovery.

Please understand you are not alone. This book proves that. It is a tool to help you understand the impact of suicide. You will be taken into the hearts and minds of those who shared their very personal stories with Heather Hays. Heather has given these stories a voice. I hope you will use them in your own healing process. I thank Heather for her commitment and courage.

My heart goes out to all those who contributed to this book and to those of you who find yourself reading it. Like me, Heather, and so many others, you may feel left behind.

—Christian C. Overton, PhD[1]

---

1. Dr. Overton has a PhD in counseling and specializes in group facilitation in industrial and organizational behavior. She also has a private consulting and coaching firm that serves businesses and nonprofit organizations.

Sealed with a Kiss
Children Left Behind

"Who Will Walk With Me?"

Holding your hand
  Walking through life

Feeling so secure
  Then in just one heartbeat

My security is gone
  Who will walk with me now?

—Kevin Johnson, Songwriter

Over the Rainbow

Imagine being four years old, cradled in your mother's arms. You are curled up next to her warm body on the couch, listening to music from *The Wizard of Oz*, reading your favorite bedtime story, *Goodnight Moon*. Everything in the house is still. It is very late, well past midnight, but you and your mother are awake, enjoying the solitude while your two brothers sleep in their rooms.

Imagining all of that is easy. Now try this:

Secure, next to your mother on that same couch, listening to the same music, you hear a loud bang at the back door. Heavy, quick footsteps make their way down the hall toward you. You instinctively move closer to your mother.

The stranger in the hallway gets closer. Then the stranger appears. He is no stranger at all. He is your father. But he doesn't look quite right. Daddy is holding a gun.

Little Elizabeth Bloy lived what some people can't even fathom. She is the four-year-old girl listening to *The Wizard of Oz* with her mother. She is the one who must live with the memory of that August night for the rest of her life.

Long before Elizabeth was born, her parents Gary and Susan Bloy dreamed of how wonderful it would be to have a family. While still dating, they talked about the perfect marriage and gorgeous children they would have. Susan believed Gary would be a supportive husband and a doting father, so when he finally proposed, she said, "Yes!"

Anticipating a future filled with love, Susan was shocked at the years following that walk down the aisle—abuse, intimidation, control. Gary also never spent much time with their children Hunter, Elizabeth, and Ramsey. In fact, when Elizabeth was born, Gary refused to believe she was his child, and for the first few months, he wouldn't even touch her.

While he never physically abused his children, they watched helplessly as he verbally abused and bullied their mother, leaving bruises on her heart and soul. Emotionally broken and financially broke, Susan was afraid the children might be Gary's next targets. She vowed to make sure that never happened.

One afternoon while Gary was at work, Susan and her children moved into a shelter for abused women. They left home with little more than the clothes on their backs. Susan knew that the most dangerous time for a woman in an abusive relationship is when she leaves, so Susan and her children stayed at the shelter until she felt they could safely be on their own.

After about four months, Susan found a home for the family—a place where they could start over without Gary. But Gary had other plans. Just a few weeks after they moved into their new home, he burst back into their lives.

On that night, he stood in the living room and stared at his wife and daughter. Gary's eyes were unfocused and glazed over. Elizabeth's blue eyes welled up with tears as she looked from the gun to her mother and then slowly to her father. She let out a blood-curdling scream, "No, Daddy, no!"

That scream brought Gary out of his trance. He bolted from the room, smashing the television with the gun as he ran out. Gary rushed out the same door he came in. He then put the gun in his mouth and pulled the trigger.

The commotion in the house was now gone. Things were once again still except for the tears and the soundtrack of *The Wizard of Oz*.

Gary Alan Bloy
Thirty-seven years old

Gary's three children, Hunter, Elizabeth, and Ramsey, each wrote him a letter two years after his death. Hunter is now eight, Elizabeth is six, and Ramsey is five.

Ramsey sat down at the kitchen table to write his letter. As soon as he was done, he watched cartoons.

> Dear Dad,
>
> I love you. I feel bad you shot yourself. I will take care of myself. I feel super-dooper bad.

When Elizabeth wrote her letter, she told her mother she was afraid of several things; she was afraid to write a letter to her dad, she was afraid he was going to shoot her and her mom, and she was afraid of how her father looked after he shot himself.

> Dear Dad,
>
> I was real scared when you killed yourself. I was scared because you had a gun. I miss you a lot. I love you.

Even though his father is gone, Hunter still tries to please him. He accepts nothing less than perfection, a pressure so great for a little boy so young.

Dear Dad,

I am mad, angry, and sad for what you did. I don't hate you for what you did, but I still wish you were alive. I'm mad and angry because you did suicide, and I'm sad because you are gone.

Dad, at school some people talk about you. For example, Stephen, he talked about you and it made me sad. Me and Stephen are rivals right now. When they have an activity for Boy Scouts, like "Dad and Lad," I can't go because I don't have a dad on earth. So I feel miserable because I'm left out. I still love you.

The children's mother and their aunt wrote much different letters to Gary. You can find their letters in "Loves Left Behind" and "Friends Left Behind."

Never-ending Story

The summer heat pouring in her bedroom window woke Linda earlier than usual. She slowly stretched and crawled out of bed. Not quite ready for the day, she went down the hall to the bathroom to get a glass of water. Then she got back into bed.

Sleep came quickly, but so did restlessness. She woke up again, this time to a closed bedroom door. Hadn't she left it open when she got her water?

"Mom!"

No answer.

"Mom?"

Still no answer. A funny feeling knotted up her stomach. The house was too quiet. She was used to hearing morning shows on television, Dad humming in the bedroom, and Mom cooking breakfast in the kitchen.

Still wearing the t-shirt she slept in, Linda walked through the house and into the backyard. No one was around, so she went to the garage to check for cars. Walking to a side door, she peaked in and looked to the left. Then she turned to the right. That moment, Linda's life began to spin out of control.

Her mother hung from the garage rafters by an extension cord. The mother of five, the wife of the same man for more than thirty years, stretched lifeless before her youngest child.

Almost three decades later, Linda can still describe what she saw. She can tell you about the stainless steel ladder standing next to her mother's body. She can tell exactly how her mother's bare feet dangled in the air. She can tell you how she screamed so loudly and ran so quickly that the neighbor who was watering his yard said it looked like her voice was trailing behind her.

Linda and her father moved more than a hundred miles away to start a new life. He tried to help them the best he could, but instead he buried himself in his work. And when Linda wanted to talk about her mother, all he would say is that her suicide was triggered by depression brought on by menopause. That's where the conversation started and stopped.

Linda craved love and she thought she found it in her high school sweetheart. She got pregnant, so they got married. She had no idea her husband, the father of her firstborn, would follow in her mother's footsteps, as would their child, Ray.

Three suicides. Thousands of questions. No answers. All that's left now is a broken-hearted woman who still needs to be held by her mother.

Betty Lou Kelly
Fifty-two years old

Dear Mom,

I sure do miss you. I wish you were still here. You have missed so much. I could have used your advice on a lot of things.

I hope you would be proud of me. I am a good mom, like you always were. I sure do love all my babies, just like you did.

Please take good care of my son, Ray. I miss him so much, but when I found out he was gone, I thought of you. I knew you would help him out. Please give him a hug for me.

Mom, I can't wait to see you again. I think about you every day. I know you were sick. No one understood what was wrong with you back then. I am so sorry you had to go through all of that.

I love you. Please wait for me.

Your daughter

Linda has also written letters to her son and husband. You can find those in "Parents Left Behind" and "Loves Left Behind."

Mr. Bear, Junior

Kelly never went to sleep without her favorite stuffed animal. "Mr. Bear" was always there to protect her—but now he protects someone else.

From the moment she was born, Kelly was "Daddy's little girl." All it took to melt the tough Texan's heart was a flash of his daughter's grin and her big hazel eyes.

Ueal Clayton showed Kelly how much he loved her every day—a kiss on the cheek at night, a cheer for the team at football games, and a scolding if Kelly needed it. Everything he did was for her.

He made Kelly so happy, she couldn't see the pain that burned deep inside her father. He was a proud man, a Marine, someone who always stood on his own. He served in Vietnam, giving perhaps the best of himself to a war that brought incredible suffering and separation.

Ueal came back from the war a changed man. He saw things no one should see. He did things no one should be asked to do. Then, just as he was trying to get his civilian life in order, he was diagnosed with paranoid schizophrenia and cancer. That's when he got hooked on pain medications.

He couldn't function without his pills. After having a leg amputated because of a war injury, he became completely introverted. He thought of himself as only a shell of the man he used to be. Kelly never saw him that way.

One of the last gifts he gave Kelly was a note pinned to "Mr. Bear." The note read: "I love you now more than ever. You will always be my little girl." Ueal left that note for his daughter just before he took his own life.

Kelly sang to her father at his funeral. She then laid "Mr. Bear" next to Ueal to be with him in heaven. "Mr. Bear" was Kelly's protector—now he would be her father's.

Ueal may be gone, but perhaps he lives on through his son-in-law. One Valentine's Day, Kelly's husband gave her a new teddy bear. Instead of holding a note, this bear was wearing diamond earrings. Kelly thought the earrings were stunning, but the bear truly touched her heart.

She sleeps with her new bear every night, never forgetting the gift of love from her husband and her father. And now, while her daddy holds "Mr. Bear," she holds "Mr. Bear, Junior."

Ueal Manuel Clayton
Fifty-two years old

Dear Daddy,

Well, I have made it almost a year without you, and let me tell you, it has been the hardest year by far. As you know, next week is my birthday. It doesn't seem worth celebrating without you.

Patrick refuses to let me not celebrate. He says my life is worth celebrating and that you are still watching me from somewhere. Mom has big plans, and I hope I can live up to acting happy about them. I just can't make people realize how significantly my life has changed without you.

Sometimes I get excited about something and I go to the phone and pick it up to call you. Then it's like hitting a brick wall because I remember you're not here. I miss you so much. I know you told me to never be a quitter, and I won't be, because my life is still worth living.

I've come to understand that maybe I was selfish: selfish for wanting to have you here in this life when you were suffering so badly. You were always so strong and you hated being dependent on anyone for anything. You were accustomed to doing things your own way. Well, you did it your way once again, and that must have taken more courage than I can imagine.

I haven't always liked the things you've done, but through it all, I have always loved you. You were my strength when I thought I couldn't go on. You always knew how to solve my problems. I can only hope that I remember half of what you taught me. Our time together was too short, and I'm envious of those near you now. I hope angels surround you and that you are no longer suffering.

The last time we talked on the phone you said, "No matter what happens, I will always be your daddy." Whether you're here or there, I will always be the luckiest woman alive because, for a short time, I had you in my life.

You left me in good hands. Patrick is a wonderful husband. Mom says that he is so much like you. So now he can hold my hand, and I will hold you in my heart forever.

I love you, and I really miss you. Until it's time for us to be together again, please watch over me.

Love always,

Daddy's little girl

Can We Call Heaven?

Tammy tucks her three young children tightly into bed. She slowly kisses each on the forehead, saying a quiet, "I love you."

DJ's soft blue eyes look up at his mother. He is seven going on twelve, and is becoming her little man more and more each day. Three-year-old Shelby snuggles with her favorite doll. With her blonde hair, freckled nose, and tanned skin, Shelby looks like a doll herself. Dereck is only two, but Tammy can already see the striking resemblance to his father, Donny. A strong chin, kind eyes, and a gentle heart. He will surely grow into an exact copy of her soul mate.

Donny used to be right beside Tammy during this bedtime routine. Both would kiss their angels gently as they drifted off to sleep. Now Tammy is a single mom. Donny took his life and left no note to explain why. Tammy has so many questions for herself and for her children. Knowing she will never find any answers, she gets by the best she can.

One of the hardest things Tammy ever had to do was explain to her children what happened to their daddy. Not wanting to frighten them, she simply told them he was in heaven.

And without even taking a breath, DJ asked, "Mommy, can we call heaven?"

With tears in her eyes, she comforted them with, "Heaven doesn't have a phone."

The children have only one way to hear their father now—in his music. Donny, a talented musician, wrote and recorded a song for Tammy. She plays it for the children every night.

The slow, soft beat begins. They hear their father strumming his guitar. They listen to the words he so devotedly sings to his wife about their children:

You gave me the three most special gifts,
They could never be replaced.
They mean so much,
As do your love and touch.

Before the children close their eyes, they blow kisses to the speakers. They look out the window at the stars and say, "We love you, Daddy."

Donald Vance Snart

Twenty-six years old

Donald's children sat down together and wrote this letter.

Dear Daddy,

We love you very much and miss you very much. You are our shining star above.

Your loving children,

DJ, Shelby, and Dereck

Gone Fishin'

His letter read simply, "I know you will forget this some day. I love you all."

My father was wrong. There is no way to forget it. Suiciders don't think about that. Their pain ends the moment they take that fatal step. Ours never does. It may lessen with time, but we never forget the way it happened. We imagine all kinds of things. What was he thinking at that last moment? Was there anything I could have done? Why didn't he say good-bye?

In my dreams, I find my dad lying on his bed—blood everywhere, his paid bills on the table, a pan still on the stove from last night's dinner, my picture on his wall. I only know that's how things looked because my brothers went to Pop's home when he died. I couldn't. I chose to remember him as I last saw him—barefoot, wearing a big smile and his favorite fishing hat.

Fishing was his passion. When we were kids he would take us to the Daytona Beach docks and we would sit there fishing for hours. He used to tease me about not wanting to bait my hook with live fish. We never caught much, but we always had a great time and great tans.

Pop's golden brown skin made him look healthy, while in reality, he was anything but. He had diabetes, emphysema, congestive heart failure, liver disease, gout, severe arthritis, and only one kidney. There wasn't a part of him that didn't hurt every day.

The last time I spoke with him was Christmas. We didn't talk very long. He just wasn't physically up to it. I meant to call him on his birthday, but didn't get the chance.

I always expected a call saying he had passed, but never expected to hear he had taken his own life. I just couldn't believe it when that call came. After all, this was the same man who spent hours talking my thirteen-year-old daughter out of taking her life. She was depressed and hopeless, and Pop explained what losing her would do to her dad and me.

I guess my dad didn't think it would be as hard on his kids, since it is natural for children to outlive their parents. But it's not natural to go that way. Life just finally took its toll on him, so he put the gun to his head.

We still go fishing, but not on the Daytona docks. Instead, I sit alone on the small bench next to his grave, on the bench with the words, "Gone Fishin'." I miss my father's smile. I miss his old hat. Most of all, I miss the man I called Pop.

Jan Fields
Vernon's Daughter

Vernon Edward Gillis
Sixty-two years old

Dear Pop,

It's been two years, three months, and sixteen days since you chose to leave us. That sounds judgmental, but it was your choice. Maybe you felt you had run out of options. I was so terribly angry with you for a long time. I felt cheated out of your time and the opportunity to say, "I love you."

You didn't talk to me before you made your decision, probably because I would have reminded you of how you talked Christina out of committing suicide. It was wrong then, and it is wrong now. I'm not speaking from a moral standpoint— more from a selfish one. Plain and simple.

You weren't around much when I was a kid, but we became close over the last ten years. I expected to make up for all those lost years, I guess. Now I won't ever get the chance.

Christina is having a hard time with it, too. She wasn't expecting Grandpa to disappear from her life that way. She called you a liar. She said all those things you said to her must have been a lie, since you "went out the same way."

I explained to her the best that I could that physical and emotional pain can cause a person to do things that he normally wouldn't do—a sort of temporary insanity. She said she understood. But I wonder.

Shannon has never been angry with you. She accepts that you were in pain and ended it after many, many years—the only way you felt you could. She's always been very understanding and forgiving. She gets that from you, I guess. She believes you are still with us. She swears you play her music box and change the channels on her television! Maybe she's right. It makes her feel better to think that way.

Over the last year I've learned to be a little more empathetic. I now know that physical and emotional pain can cause one's mind to think of all sorts of ways to end things. I wish you could have come up with another plan, but there's no point in going on about something I have no power to change.

I just want you to know that we love you and miss you terribly, and hopefully, one day, we'll see you again. We have some catching up to do. Pop, I love you!

Hugs and Kisses,

Jan

All My Loving

S hannon walked down the sidewalk toward her front porch. A business card was stuck in the metal frame of the screen door. The teen was just getting home from school and her parents weren't home from work yet. As she reached for the card, she froze. It was from the coroner's office. The handwritten message read, "Call about Stan Pratt." That's how Shannon found out her father was dead.

She and her older brother, Scott, arranged the funeral and memorial services. Their parents had been married twenty-two years and their mother, Sarah, was too depressed to handle the details.

Stan had been suffering mentally and emotionally, but no one expected him to take his life. He had injured his back while loading a cement truck ten years earlier. He then went through several extremely painful back surgeries and rehabilitation.

Eventually, doctors could do nothing more for Stan. He would have to take pills every day for the rest of his life to stop the pain. After a decade of living like that, he could not imagine going through it one more day—let alone a lifetime. So he drove to a drug store, refilled his prescriptions, and took all of the pills as he sat alone in his car in the parking lot.

That may have been Stan Pratt's last day on this earth, but it is not how his family remembers him. They remember the man who got a kick out of wrestling with the kids in the backyard, who lived for NASCAR and Dale Earnhardt, who could answer any question about the Beatles, and who fell in love with his wife Sarah at the age of sixteen.

They also remember one particular Father's Day. Sarah told Stan that the children had packed up some old clothes to give to the needy. She asked him to go through the clothes to make sure there was nothing he wanted. At the bottom of the pile was a leather Beatles jacket. It had song titles and the faces of the Fab Four all over it.

Stan giggled and laughed, so surprised and excited. He refused to take off the jacket, even when he went to bed that night. That's the man the Pratt family remembers—the man who wore a big smile the night he fell asleep wearing a Beatles jacket.

Stan Dean Pratt
Forty years old

Dad,

I am sorry I didn't talk to you on Father's Day. I tried. The lines were busy. I figured we would talk later. The days flew by, and I never got to tell you, "I'm sorry." It was your last Father's Day with us.

I forgive you for what you did, but I will never understand why. I might not have told you what a great dad you were and how much I love you, but you were a great dad, and I do love you. I miss you a lot.

Love, your son,

Scott

Dad,

Well, a couple of years have passed now, but I still think of you every day. I think of the good times we had together and the moments you have missed in my life.

I cherish the nineteen years that I had such a wonderful dad. You were my best friend, and I miss you so much. My world will never be the same without you, but you made it a better place by being in it.

I try to make the joy of having had you in my life take away the pain of losing you. I don't want to be selfish, but I need you here. You are my dad. You are supposed to be here for me.

It is still hard to accept that you chose to die. I thought your love for me would take away any problems in your life.

I was wrong. I know you are in a better place and no longer in pain. That alone allows me to accept your decision.

I will always love you,

Shannon

Sounds of the Season

The house was alive with the aroma of fresh pine and homemade pumpkin pie. A newly cut Christmas tree stood tall in the corner of the living room, wrapped presents were displayed proudly underneath, and a long grocery list for their traditional Christmas dinner lay on the kitchen table. It was a wonderful snapshot of a Norman Rockwell afternoon. That picture didn't last long. The Fetterolf family portrait that Christmas season would be stained with tragedy and tears.

The hot Texas sun shone brightly through the window. Dave's wife, children, and grandchildren were in the kitchen, busily making plans for the holiday meal. No one noticed that Dave had been absent for quite some time—not until a loud bang caused them to stop talking mid-sentence. The silence was as loud as the chatter left hanging in the air.

The bang sent a chill through Dave's son, Troy. Despite the urge to stay right where he was, Troy ran toward the noise. He found his father slumped over on the concrete floor of the garage, dead at the age of fifty-six, from a self-inflicted gunshot wound. Just thirty-six days later, Troy would leave his family as well. Finding his father dead was the beginning of his end.

Dave's suicide is the sad fact of how his life ended. But that does not reflect who he was—a good husband, a loving father, a faithful friend, and a solid provider. Dave and his wife raised a happy family. Active in the community, he was one of the most well-liked men on the block. His yard was perfectly manicured, his cars were always clean, his wife was pretty, and his children were well behaved.

He loved his children and grandchildren with all of his heart and would do anything for them, especially on holidays. Halloween meant that Grandpa dressed up and passed out candy. Valentine's Day included kisses and chocolate hearts. But the Christmas season was Dave's favorite time of year. Shortly before he died, he arranged for a visit from Santa for the children.

So what made this hard-working and easy-loving man take his life just days before Christmas, while the family he cared so much for was only a hundred feet away? Dave was a manic depressive and an alcoholic, two things he tried very hard to hide. On the day his family followed that heart-breaking bang into the garage, he could hide no more. His dark secrets defeated him. Dave lay there, lifeless, his blood alcohol level twice the legal limit.

Neither illness had mattered to Dave's family. They knew he was a big-hearted man with a great laugh and an even greater smile. He was kind and gentle, generous and caring. He just had no idea how much he was loved and how much his leaving would hurt his family.

They were all very close, but Dave and Troy had a special bond—one that brought them closer than most fathers and sons. They spent countless weekend hours golfing, when they would talk about everything from sports to the outdoors to dating. Neither cared much about who had the best score. Dave usually won, but if he didn't, he would say that he let his son win. The two even spent the workweek together. Troy worked for his father, and Dave always announced that Troy was his favorite employee.

Both men fought personal battles with the bottle. Troy managed to stay sober for eight months before his father's death. But after his death, he just couldn't face life without his best friend. Five weeks after Dave suicided, Troy, at the age of twenty-nine, accidentally overdosed. He died in his sleep.

When Dave pulled the trigger that December day, he shattered his life, his son's life, and the lives of his family and friends. When his grandchildren ask how Grandpa died, their mother says, "Grandpa died of a broken heart." The same can be said for Troy.

Christmas will never be the same. But as time passes, the guilt and grief lessen to a dull throb rather than a stabbing pain. The Fetterolf family still aches for Dave and Troy, and for the Norman Rockwell images of days gone by. Now all they have are stories and photographs of Christmases past.

Dave Fetterolf
Fifty-six years old

Dear Dad,

This letter is so hard for me to write. I miss you so much. I can't believe it has been two and a half years since you died. I just want you to know how incredibly much you are missed! I think about you so often. Sometimes I see a man's hands and they remind me of you. You always seemed so strong.

Sometimes I hear a man laugh and the sound brings back powerful memories of your loud and crazy laugh. I remember all the fun times we had together. I had this dream of you once. It was so real, I felt as though you were with me. I woke up happy because I got to see you one more time.

My son Brad has your laugh. I smile when I hear him because I feel like a part of you lives on in your grandson. We still draw straws to see who has to sit by him at the movies! Sound familiar? He has your round, smiling face and your kind and tender heart. You would be so proud of him, Dad. He got the "Heart of the Lion" award this year at school. He has really grown up. When I look at him, I see so much of you! That makes me happy.

Kelsey, still feisty, excels at every sport, and was even valedictorian this year. She is a switch-hitter in baseball and has taken up golf again. She plans on getting a basketball scholarship to SMU. She remembers when you took her for her first golf lessons. She is so loving and sweet.

Lindsey is blossoming, too. She is as smart as a whip, and has a sprinkling of freckles across her nose. Everyone says she looks just like me. I am so sad you didn't get to know her better. I am sad that she won't have you in her life as long as I did.

I have a really hard time at Father's Day. I just want you to know you were such a great dad. You were a wonderful person. I wish I could have you back for just one more day. Just one more hug. Just one more, "I love you."

I'll never forget you, Dad. I pray you are at peace with the Lord. Give Troy a big hug for me. We miss him so much, too.

Our family was forever changed, but the love remains strong and hopeful. I look forward to the day we are reunited, and I thank God for the faith that has brought me through this. I miss you, and I love you.

Your daughter,

Michelle

Hidden Treasures

So often a person's true worth goes unnoticed—her unique gifts overlooked. Not until someone is gone do we recognize what they had to offer. Funny how Karen always saw good in the world around her, but not in herself.

Karen was an odd mix. She was as bold as a bulldog, ready to tear into anyone who meant trouble, yet with family and friends, she was as gentle as a light breeze blowing across a field. Beneath the smoking, drinking, laying-it-all-on-the-line woman was a compassionate single mom of two precious baby girls. Karen worked her fingers raw to keep a roof over their heads and clothes on their backs. But she hadn't always been that tough.

Karen left high school and got married right away with hopes of a better life. She didn't find one. Physically abused by her husband, she felt trapped, scared, and alone, with no one to turn to. The man Karen thought would protect her instead destroyed her dignity and tried to break her spirit. His abuse escalated out of control the night he shot her while she was three months pregnant with her daughter, Tracy. Still, torn between love and hate for the father of her unborn daughter, Karen didn't leave. The physical wounds healed, although her heart never did.

Tracy spent the first few years of her life watching her mother suffer beatings at the hands of her father. Tracy was angry and frightened, with overwhelming feelings of guilt and frustration. How could a little girl understand?

But Tracy did understand, and was thankful when her mother finally walked out the door. Her mother hid her tears with courage and conviction, packed up Tracy and her little sister Kim, and left, not knowing where they would go. She only knew she wanted something better for her daughters.

Karen did show her girls a better life. She went back to school and graduated with straight A's. She married a man who treated her and her children with kindness and compassion. Together they built a home filled with love and affection. Karen also showed her daughters what she was really made of. She gave them unconditional love and proved she was one heck of a do-it-yourselfer. They watched her remodel their home, install plumbing, fix a car, sew, cook, and garden. You name it, Karen did it.

One of her other passions was antiquing. She would go on day-long road trips with her daughters to out-of-the-way shops and find beautiful pieces overlooked by others. Karen had a way of spotting something unique, something that just needed some tender loving care.

Like her antiques, Karen was extraordinary. So, why, on that January morning, she felt she could no longer move forward, no one can understand. The only thing Tracy knows for sure is that her mother was a woman to be admired. And she wishes her mother had received as much tender loving care as she gave everyone and everything around her.

Karen Elaine Rodgers O'Neal
Forty-seven years old

Hi Mom,

I went to the lake today. You know, the lake we put half of your ashes in after you died? The drive always reminds me of when my sister called to tell me she found you in your garage. I pinched my hand to make sure it wasn't a dream. I couldn't feel the pinch because I was so numb. I remember seeing you before they took you away. I wanted to crawl in your lap and have you hold me. That was two and a half years ago.

Today, I went to the lake for fun. I didn't know if I could ever go again with a smile on my face, but guess what? I can. You taught me to be strong. And I am.

Your suicide took away a year of my life. You were all I thought about all day, every day. I still think of you, but your suicide no longer consumes me.

I went with my husband to the lake. You never liked him, but he is still with me, and you aren't. My four-year-old little boy, who was just one when you died, was also with me. You would love him so much. He is so smart and tender-hearted. He often talks about you, his grandma in heaven.

Anyway, we went out on our new boat. Grandpa still has your boat. I wish you would have bought a newer one or could at least be here to enjoy ours. The water is too cold to ski or tube, but we wade in it. I didn't think I could ever step foot in that water after we put some of your ashes in it, but I can.

I don't go to your grave much anymore. We put your other ashes there so we could take you flowers. We took you some on Mother's Day. I get angry that I have to visit you there, so I usually just don't go.

I went on Mother's Day out of respect for you and because my sister wanted me to. You would be so proud of her. She has made it through her first year of nursing school with honors. Graduation is going to be so bittersweet. Her heart will break when she looks out and sees all of the proud moms. Your face will not be there.

Speaking of your face, sometimes I just can't see it anymore. Other times I see it plain as day. You will always live in my heart and memories, but I hope your death continues to lose its hold on me, and that one day all I remember is how much I love you.

Love always, your daughter,

Tracy

My Grandma

New Year's Eve is always a special night. The old year is behind us, and a fresh beginning is ahead. It's a time to rediscover what we want and what we expect from ourselves, a time to reflect on the good and to learn from the bad.

Karen always loved New Year's Eve, especially the one that brought the birth of her grandson, Austin. He was the light of her life. They were as close as any two people could be. Their eyes sparkled when they looked at each other.

Karen lived in a home by a lake and had a small pond just outside her front door. She had a wonderful green thumb and surrounded the pond with lush plants and colorful flowers. Austin and his grandma spent much of their time in that paradise.

Karen took her life just five days after Austin turned eight. After suffering years of emotional and physical abuse, the pain was too much. She was hurting, and nothing, not even her love for Austin, could keep her here. She had his picture with her when she died.

She went to a paradise outside the pond in her yard. She left for a place where every day is New Year's Eve, where there are always new beginnings, and where nothing can hurt her again.

Karen Elaine Rodgers O'Neal

Forty-seven years old

My name is Austin, and I want to tell you about my grandma. Her name was Karen O'Neal. She liked to use her magical hands for gardening, and she had a Chihuahua named Ginger. And she liked to cook, too.

We were close, and I always stayed with her. I wish she were a living person. When I found out my grandma died, I was miserable because I didn't have my friend to go to the lake with and fish with. I always liked to show her how good I could fish.

My mommy told me that my grandma killed herself. I was shocked, and I thought she did it because she thought she did something bad. I went to a camp to help me learn about someone dying in my family, and it helped me a lot. I hope people will try to get help and not kill themselves, because it makes us very sad when they do. I love and miss my grandma.

Austin Reid

Eight years old

Remembering New Year's

The US Marshall and his daughter stood on the roof of the San Francisco federal building, holding dozens of calendars. They had gone from desk to desk collecting those calendars. Now they listened to the pages flutter in the wind as they waited for the right moment to start their private party.

Melissa Anne squinted in the afternoon sun as she soaked up the glorious city. Her father looked at her and smiled, and together they began the countdown.

They shouted into the wind, "Ten, nine, eight . . ."

Barely able to stand still, Melissa Anne was on her tiptoes, ready to send the old year out with their own ticker-tape parade.

"Three, two, one! Happy New Year!"

And with that, those calendars went flying! The old year soared from the top of the building, the calendars twisting and turning, sometimes climbing higher before beginning the descent.

Melissa Anne's little-girl giggle and her father's deep, genuine laugh filled the afternoon air. They danced in a circle at their own New Year's Eve party.

Dennis Berry and his daughter then hurried down to his twentieth-floor office. They stood at the window and watched the days and months swirl through the air. The sunshine reflecting off the white pages sent out random flashes of bright colors. Dennis and Melissa Anne stood there until the last page landed below.

To top off their celebration, they wrote down their New Year's resolutions and promised to keep each other on track. They hung those lists on Dennis's bulletin board. Then, holding hands, the two quietly left the building and drove home.

That was their annual New Year's celebration. No one else was on the roof. No one else tossed those calendars. No one else watched the fireworks of colors given off by the pages as they floated to the street.

Melissa Anne's fondest memories of her father are of those New Year's Eves. They shared the holiday together; now it's hers alone. The only other person who was there is dead.

Because Dennis had such a tender heart with his family, you would never know he was responsible for capturing some of the country's most dangerous fugitives. Once, during a visit to her father's office, Melissa Anne became one of those fugitives. Dennis pretended to book her and her Cabbage Patch Kids Gang on bank robbery charges. Melissa Anne and her gang were given a crime file and fingerprinted. She still has that crime file.

Melissa Anne's hero put the bad guys behind bars so that she, her mother, and her brother could sleep soundly at night. After her father took his life, sleeping soundly became a thing of the past. Melissa Anne was a teenager when he died, but she still hoped he would come walking down the hall to tuck her in or sing her to sleep.

When she did sleep, she never went to a peaceful place. She had nightmares she prayed would end. She wanted her father to call, to send a letter, to ring the doorbell. But none of those things would ever happen again.

Why had he ended his life? Was he unhappy in his new marriage? Was he sad that he was living thousands of miles away from his two children? Was he drinking too much? Those questions can only be answered when Melissa Anne sees her father again. For now, she has to be satisfied with her memories. She looks through her crime file and smiles.

She also smiles when she thinks about their calendar countdowns. Melissa Anne doesn't throw calendars from the top of that building anymore. But once a year, when the clock strikes midnight, she says a silent, "Happy New Year" to the man who gave her such special memories.

Dennis Michael Berry
Forty-six years old

Dear Daddy,

I miss you more than you will ever know. You left me at a time in my life when I needed you most. I was only sweet sixteen.

Almost ten years later, I still think about you every day. I don't think you thought about what this would do to us because you wouldn't have left us that way if you did.

I am mad at you for it, yet I still love you very much. You have missed so many important things. I graduated from high school, started college to be a police officer like you, and then changed my mind.

I also got married. You were supposed to walk your little girl down the aisle. Instead, my brother did. You now have two beautiful grandchildren who will only know you through stories and pictures. How I wish you could meet them. Seryna has your eyes and Noah has your face. When I look at them, I see so much of you.

I never dealt with your leaving. Now that I have a family of my own, I want to deal with it. I want to have our memories of when you were here. They seem to be slipping away, and I don't want that. It's like there is a block inside, not letting me remember until I come to terms with this. So that's what I am going to do.

I miss you calling me Liz. Now my brother does, and he sounds just like you. I miss you, Dad. Not a day will ever go by that I don't think of you. I wish I could see you one last time, but that is one wish that won't come true. I love you with all my heart, Daddy.

Loving you, forever "Daddy's little girl,"

Melissa Anne

Changing Face of Father

Like something out of a television movie that wasn't supposed to happen in real life—to me or anyone else—things started to change. I am not sure when. All I know is, they did.

Were my eyes closed to it? Did I not want to see the bad in my family? We lived in an upper-class neighborhood on a tree-lined street with large yards. We were not rich by any means, but we never went without. Now I live without one of my parents.

My father, Bert Koehler III, died by his own hand. But there is so much more to him than just his death. He was a wonderful man and an extremely giving father. Things were not always as bad as they were in those last few years.

My father became a sick man. I think anyone who resorts to suicide is not healthy in his mind. He tried to hide his illness, even from himself, and we never realized the degree of his depression. A tiny island in the middle of a vast, lonely, flowing ocean, he put up a wall that no one could penetrate. Knowing what I know now, I wish I could go back and do many things differently. But then again, don't we all want that?

My parents were in the middle of a divorce after twenty-six years of marriage. My father did not want the divorce, even though he and my mother had grown apart. Every breakup has its dark side; theirs was no different.

During that turbulent time, my parents lived in the same house but kept different bedrooms. The tension was incredible. I was twenty-three and living with them. My two younger brothers, nineteen and sixteen, were also there.

I remember coming home from work one Wednesday, and, as usual, I went up to my room to correct some of my students' assignments. Around five o'clock, I heard what had become a familiar sound—another argument. Screaming filled the house. I tried to stay out of my parents' fights, but I always stood by in case they needed a referee.

My nineteen-year-old brother and I listened from my bedroom door as the fight entered unfamiliar territory. We could hear things being thrown around their bedroom. I heard glass breaking and my mom screaming.

The fight moved into the upstairs hall. My parents were face-to-face, almost touching, as they yelled, cursed, and belittled each other. Then my dad shoved my mom. At only 5'2", she sailed through the air and down the stairs until she was stopped by the wall near the front door. The next thing I knew, a string of obscenities was being hurled at my dad. Then I realized I was the one doing the screaming.

My father shrunk back as I yelled, "Are you happy now?"

I ran to call 911. My brother ran to my unconscious mother. Dad walked down the stairs past his injured wife, in shock at what his anger and illness had done.

What happened next was even worse. My youngest brother walked into the house just as our father stabbed a kitchen knife into his own chest. My brother stood there, stunned.

The next few minutes stretched out like hours. So many sirens, so much activity. A whirlwind blew through as I watched my father being taken out of the house on a stretcher. He had given up. He wanted to die because he believed he had killed his wife.

But I couldn't let him go so easily. I rushed past the officer who was trying to hold me back. He told me not to go outside. Somehow I knew in my heart that that would be the last time I would see my dad alive. His eyes gazed blankly up at the sky. He lay so helpless and frail on that stretcher, but for one small moment I know he saw me standing over him.

The ambulance carried my father away. He and my mom went to the hospital, while the rest of us went to the police station. Detectives questioned us all, even my mom, after she was released from the hospital.

All I remember while giving my statement was the sun setting outside the window. I sat in the room for hours with a total stranger thinking, "What a glorious sunset. It's a glorious sunset, and my dad is probably dead."

We got word of my father's passing hours later, while we were still at the police station. We had all gathered in the room where we had been interrogated. My mother walked in and told us the news.

Years later, the family is still struggling to comprehend something no one can explain. I am still waiting to wake up from this nightmare. In this world where nothing seems normal, I have only one wish: that one day my dad will hear me say, "I love you."

Pidge Koehler
Bert's Daughter

Herbert "Bert" Koehler III

Fifty-two years old

Oh, Dad, why did you have to go?
    It wasn't your time yet, didn't you know?
In an instant you were gone,
    With one push of the kitchen knife,
My last glimpse of you on the lawn.
    Words cannot express what I need to say.
Yes, every day I pay
    For my silence and the violence.
Oh, the anger and the rage
    That was so deep within.
We were all in a cage.
    The dad I adored had gone far away.
I was so afraid to move toward this monster
    Here to stay.
My last memory of you
    Is seeing your eyes so blue
Look up at the sky
    As they wheeled you away to die.
Dad, I say this now,
    Hoping that you will hear,
I love and miss you.
    Should've said it when I had the chance.
Wish you were there for my wedding day,
    Daddy-daughter dance.
As I wish this for you:
    My eye drops a tear,
I hope, Daddy Dear,
    You love me, too.

Pidge Koehler

Waking Up

I was eighteen years old when my father and I began to have a good relationship. I was also eighteen when he suicided. I spent years feeling guilty, until the morning I finally woke up.

My father came to visit shortly after his wife passed away. He was supposed to stay for two weeks, but ended up staying only four days. That was when he took his life.

I felt responsible for his death. I should have seen how depressed he was. In fact, during his visit, I remember asking him not to do anything stupid, and he said he wouldn't. Because of that promise, I didn't think he would suicide, no matter how depressed he was. I didn't realize that to him, suicide was not stupid. So in his mind, he wasn't lying to me.

It wasn't until more than five years later that I let go of my guilt. I can't really explain exactly what happened except to say my father came to see me in a dream.

In my dream I saw how depressed he was, and I wanted to do anything to help him. He confided in me that he was seriously thinking about suiciding. I begged him not to do it. I told him that with time, and perhaps counseling, things would get better. However, he was too impatient to wait.

I asked him to give me the full two weeks of his visit to see if I could help him get through his depression. He said he would. We did a lot of talking and really got to know each other. But after only a few days, he began reminding me how little time he had left in his visit.

I would always respond, "Dad, please give me a chance and keep an open mind."

He would just smile and walk away.

Dad didn't stay with me the fourteen days he promised. He gave me only four. That's when he said, "Christy, you've done the best you could do, and I appreciate it. It means a lot to me that you wanted to try, but it just didn't work. I'm sorry, but I can't live like this any longer."

He drove us to the deserted spot he had already chosen. We both walked around for a while. I started crying and said, "Dad, I'm sorry if I let you down or disappointed you."

He replied, "You didn't. This is something I have to do. I have been dead for a long time. I'm tired and drained."

After I told him I understood, I began to walk away, but quickly turned back and said, "I can't let you do this. If you're going to take your life, you're going to have to take mine, too."

We both cried. He finally agreed to take me with him. We sat down and he put his arm around me. He put the gun to his head. My dream became a nightmare.

"I'm going to count to five and when I do, it will all be over."

All I heard was, "One, two, three . . ."

Everything happened in slow motion. I saw the gun drop out of his hand and felt him falling back, pulling me with him. Our bodies collapsed. Everything went dark. Then I opened my eyes and saw him stand up and walk away from me.

"Dad, please don't go! Don't leave me!"

"Christy, my time is up, but yours isn't. The ambulance is on its way to get you. You will be fine. I have to go. You did everything you could, but this was a battle I had to fight. I gave up a long time ago. I will always watch over you."

I woke up from that dream crying. Such a long time had passed since I had dreamt about my father. But for the first time since he died, I felt some peace. I know some people won't believe it, but my dad was with me that night. He was there to help me deal with my guilt.

I finally understood that I could not have pulled him out of his depression. Only he could do that. I might have been able to help him—if he had allowed me to—but I know he is finally at peace with himself. I miss him terribly, but I must move forward. My dad would not want me to feel guilty for the rest of my life.

Christine Stone-Monaghan
David's Daughter

David Jon Stone
Forty years old

Dear Dad,

Life around here has been so crazy without you. So much has happened in the last eight years. I wish you could have been here to share some of the events with me. Some were good, but some have been really hard. I have missed you so much.

I have two beautiful little girls now. I wish you could be here to see them. It's hard to think of you as a grandfather. What would that have been like? For a long time, I felt like "Daddy's little girl." Something tells me that they would have been "Grandpa's little girls." They are both so beautiful and smart.

My life has changed so much. I have been divorced and remarried. Dylan is a wonderful man. He is very good to me and is supportive. You would have liked him.

School was important to you. I felt as if I let you down by not finishing high school and going to college. But guess what? I have now finished my first year at the community college. Dylan will graduate with a master's when I graduate with my associate's degree.

From there, I am going to go on to a university. You would be so proud of me. My dream is to get a PhD in psychology. I would like nothing more than to have you at my graduation. Even though you will be there in spirit, I still wish you could be there in person.

Remember when we went bowling, but we didn't bowl? We sat and ate lunch and talked for hours. We had never just talked before. I really enjoyed spending that time together. I always wanted some time alone with you, and had never really had that before. Thank you so much for giving me those few hours of undivided attention. It meant so much to me.

I have never been angry with you. I know you did not suicide to hurt me or because you didn't love me. Even if you didn't tell me you loved me often, I know you did.

I think about you every day. After losing you, I thought my entire world had collapsed. The only thing that helped me get through this loss was knowing that at least you were no longer hurting.

I hope I have made you proud. I have worried about that. I know you will be with me wherever I go. Sometimes I can almost feel you with me. I promise to do my best in life. I hope you know that I will always love you.

Love,

Christine

Help to Heal a Child's Heart

A broken-hearted child is a tragedy. Children should wear smiles, not sadness. When Mom or Dad suicides, a young child learns the realities of life and death, while he or she should still be learning how to read. Being an adult when a parent suicides does not help one better understand why it happened. No matter what a person's chronological age, losing a parent takes us all back to childhood. Parents are the foundation of the family. It is the natural order of things for them to leave this earth before their children—but not by suicide.

Being the survivor brings feelings of shame and anger. Hunter was only eight years old when he wrote a letter to his father Gary (see "Over the Rainbow"), and he clearly expresses these emotions through his words. Many children and teens may believe if they had behaved properly, gotten better grades in school, or had not made Daddy mad, he would not have suicided. They may believe saying their prayers every night, doing their chores, or not rebelling would have made Mommy happier, so she would not have suicided. Austin writes about his loss in "My Grandma" revealing just how confusing suicide is for a child.

Never is one individual able to determine another's fate, yet blame and guilt are common. If a parent puts a gun to his or her head, as Christine's father did in "Waking Up," some may blame the gun manufacturers and lack of gun control. In a poem to her father, Pidge writes, "Every day I pay for my silence," a sign of guilt for something she could not control (see "Changing Face of Father").

You are not to blame. Your parent made a personal decision that had nothing to do with you. Like a wound, your pain will leave a scar, but you will survive and grow. So how do you cope? There are steps you can take to ease your pain:

- **Talk**—Talk to your friends, your teacher, your coach, or your counselor. Talking keeps you in touch with others. You can even talk to your parent who suicided. Tell your mom or dad how you feel.

- **Read**—Read about the experiences of others who have lost a parent. Read for relaxation and enjoyment, even just a page or two. Pick up a new comic book or coloring book. How about a book that seems like a guilty pleasure?

- **Do something good for yourself**—Maybe you can take a long walk on the beach, or have a picnic, or enjoy a long bath. Be kind to yourself. Spend the night with a friend, or go to the pet shelter to make a four-legged friend.

- **Laugh**—Watch a comedy. Do something that makes you laugh. You don't need to feel bad for not feeling sad all the time. No one will criticize you for laughing.

- **Write or draw**—Get a journal, tablet, or drawing pad. Put feelings, pictures, thoughts, and scribbles on paper. Be spontaneous. Write freely without over thinking your ideas. E-mail one of the people in this book who has been left behind. Share your thoughts and feelings. E-mail addresses are listed in the back of the book for that very purpose.

- **Gravitate toward your favorite things**—This might be a teddy bear, like Kelly had in "Mr. Bear, Junior." Or maybe your dad had a baseball glove you can play with. Maybe your mom had a favorite cookbook you can now use for your recipes. Keep your parent's ring or watch in your pocket. Pull it out when you are lonely.

- **Cry**—If you need to cry, do it. It may seem uncomfortable at first, but go ahead and do it. But don't feel guilty if you don't cry. Some of us cry more easily than others.

- **Create a memory book**—A book can help you document your parent's life. Include photos, old ticket stubs to concerts or movies, or travel brochures from vacations. If you are helping a child heal, make a memory book together. As the child grows up, the book may help him or her remember the parent a little more clearly. If you are an adult who lost a parent, the memory book will be a treasure to pass on to your children so they can know their grandparent.

- **Ask for help**—You do not need to suffer alone. You can ask for help. Talk to a therapist, find a crisis center in your neighborhood, or go to your church. Seeking help does not mean you are weak. And in the end, it can make you stronger.

All of the strange and confusing emotions you are feeling are normal. Grief is an individual experience, and from it, you will grow. As you read the stories in this book, allow the healing to begin. Allow these stories to empower you. You have been left behind, but you are not alone. May God bless you on your journey.

Linda Runnells[1]
Counselor

---

1. Linda Runnells is a licensed professional counselor, currently in private practice in Wharton, Texas. She has worked in the mental health field for more than twenty years, with clients from all backgrounds, but her first love is working with children and families. She has three children and six grandchildren, and has been married to her high school sweetheart for almost forty years.

When the Bough Breaks
Parents Left Behind

"Tell Me"

Tell me where you are tonight
Tell me that you're safe
Tell me that you love me
It must be a mistake

—Eileen Shaw
Brendan's Mother
Brendan suicided at twenty years old

Garden of Angels

"No, no, no! Not my Shaun!"

Johan tried to hold his screaming wife, but Sandra punched and kicked at him, at the walls, at everyone and everything. Not until her doctor arrived and filled her with enough tranquilizers to knock out a large man did she begin to calm down. As her body slowed, Sandra's mind raced. Flashing back a year and half, she cried, "Not again!"

South Africa had been especially cold that winter. Sandra had been putting on an extra sweater when she turned and saw her oldest boy, Robby, standing in her bedroom doorway.

"Mom, I'm sorry. I don't want you to suffer anymore."

He pointed the revolver at his head.

"No, Robby, no!"

A deafening bang filled the air. Her son fell to the floor. He whispered, "Mommy," the first and last word Robby ever spoke.

He had looked like a little boy sleeping. His face was peaceful, his spirit calm. But Robby wasn't a little boy, and he wasn't sleeping. He was dead at the age of twenty-one from a self-inflicted gunshot wound.

Sandra stared down at her firstborn, her head spinning as she fell to her knees. In seconds, her mind rushed from the bloodstained carpet to the first time she had held her baby.

Stanley "Robby" Thompson, named after his father, was born on a sunny March day in Johannesburg. Sandra believed this baby boy would make her family perfect. In reality, her family life was anything but perfect. The best words to describe her eleven-year marriage were "humiliating" and "extremely violent." There were daily fights between Sandra and Stanley that left her covered with bruises, cuts, and scars.

Robby was only two when he saw his father throw Sandra on the bed and stand over her, pointing a gun at her head. Just before he pulled the trigger, Robby jumped onto the bed, covered his mother's head with his arms, and pushed the gun away. The little boy yelled, "You cannot shoot my mom!" That was the first sentence Robby ever spoke.

Robby was his mother's hero, always trying to stop his father from hurting her, although he was seldom successful. When his brother Shaun was born, Robby tried to protect him as well. Shaun, so young and small compared to his overbearing alcoholic father, usually hid in a corner and watched in terror.

After more than a decade of abuse, Sandra finally left Stanley. She married Johan about three years later. He did his best to provide her and the boys with a loving, stable home. He wanted to be the father the boys never had. But it wasn't easy for any of them. The boys had been through so much.

There were happy times in the new family, but both boys had deep emotional scars. Not until shortly before Robby took his life did he tell his mother he had nightmares about the times his father beat her. He remembered her being hit and even stabbed. Sandra never knew he had those memories.

As Robby lay dying at her feet, Sandra fully understood all the pain her son had suffered. She wanted to hold him, to breathe life back into him, to tell him it would be okay. But Robby was gone. He took his life three days before Shaun's nineteenth birthday.

Now, just before Christmas, Shaun was gone as well. Sandra's thoughts were swirling, the tranquilizer taking effect, her mind replaying a life filled with heartache and desperation, abuse and disappointment.

She buried Shaun next to Robby and slowly tried to put the pieces of this tragedy together. Sandra learned from Shaun's friends that he talked a lot about Robby. That surprised her, because after Robby's death, Shaun never mentioned his name to her again.

Shaun told his friends that he was very much alone in the world. Isolated and confused, Shaun's greatest wish was to be with his big brother. By his own hand, he made his wish come true.

Sandra's only comfort now is knowing her boys are together. Her little boys. Her heroes. Her guardian angels.

Stanley "Robby" Thompson
Twenty-one years old

Shaun Edward Thompson
Twenty years old

"If"

If I could have you back as sweet little angel babies once more, I would never put you down. I would just hold you in my arms and look at your sweet baby faces. I would just kiss your little rosebud noses and rosy cheeks.

If I could have you back as sweet toddlers, busy as little bees once more, I would never get impatient with all the "whys." I would sit down on the floor with you and play cars and blocks and read you stories every day. I would treasure all the crumpled flowers you gave me with dirty little toddler hands and all the sticky hugs and kisses, too.

If I could have you back as lovely, lively, energetic teenagers once more, I would never ask you to come back later when I'm not busy. If you wanted to discuss something, I would listen and bear with your loud music and even go skateboarding with you. I would hug and kiss you much more often, because even if you acted like you didn't like it, I know now that you needed it.

If I could have you back as beautiful, grown-up young men once more, I would never assume that you did not need all the guidance and support I gave you as children. I would never assume that you could cope through difficult times. I would really try and be a better "grown-up Mommy."

If...

Sandra Marx

Mother to Robby and Shaun

A River So Deep

Louisiana summers are too hot for long sleeves, but Trena was rarely seen in anything but long sleeves. She was sixteen and had freckles, frizzy brown hair, and a fast tongue. A middle child adored by her older brother and admired by her younger sister, she had an innocent and curious beauty. But she got lost somewhere along the winding road from childhood to womanhood.

Trena Lee Grimmett's mother sits alone in their backyard garden now, remembering their time together in the fragrance of the flowers. An occasional breeze cooled down their afternoon conversations. She thinks of their walks to the town's library, where Trena would soak up stories from Christian-based books. Books that offered teens hope and guidance on issues like peer pressure, pregnancy, and abuse.

Trena needed that guidance when she lost a dear cousin to suicide. She struggled to understand her cousin's pain, but trying to comprehend the impossible was out of reach for the ten-year-old.

Trena's mother never truly realized how much her daughter struggled. One would never know by looking at her how much she suffered inside. She was so talented, an award-winning photographer who was happiest when capturing instant images of life. The face of an old woman. Children laughing in the rain. The setting sun.

But as Trena's passion for photography grew, the snapshot of her own life darkened. Her life became a transparency of what it once was—a change in friends, a change in feelings, a change in fashion.

That fashion now included Gothic clothing or anything that hid her body. She wore long sleeves so no one could see how she cut her arms. Her creative canvas had turned from the camera's lens to her own body. She cut to gain control.

Trena's parents did all they could to stop her downward slide. They turned to the church for help, locked Trena in her room, and eventually sent her to boarding school. At times, her family was hopeful—at others, hopeless. One minute Trena would be in counseling and in church, vowing to change. The next, she would sneak out of school.

Not until after her death did Trena's parents learn that she told school counselors she had suffered a miscarriage after being raped. Her parents will never know if that truly happened or if Trena was crying for help. Just nine days after her sixteenth birthday, Trena made the loudest cry of all. Two years of depression took over, and she took her life.

Trena's mother still sits on the porch. She sips her mint tea and takes in the summer symphony. The birds sing. The bees hum. The wind blows through the trees. It seems like yesterday that Trena sat beside her, a book in one hand and her mother's hand in the other. But then again, that wasn't yesterday, and those Louisiana summers are too hot for long sleeves.

Trena Lee Grimmett
Sixteen years old

These are journal entries written by Trena's mother, Charlene.

One month after Trena's death—
>I miss you so very much, and I am so angry at what you did! But I am not angry with you. I love you, and I'm glad you are in the arms of God. When my mind wanders away from the cross, I get very upset thinking about you. I must walk closer to the Lord.

Pray for me, Trena. Your sister had a bad dream last night and wanted to sleep with us awhile. No problem. I remember another little girl who would do the same thing. I miss you. I went to the doctor, and he put me on antianxiety medication.

Two months after her death—

Good morning, Trena. I love you. I have begun to read some books on surviving a suicide. Some of the revelations are that you became so sick with depression that you died. The way one dies from depression is suicide. The chemicals in your brain were out of balance, and that caused you to view the world as a place too painful to live in.

Three months after her death—

One day I will run to hold you in my arms again. What is death like? I wish you could tell me. Another first has come and gone. My birthday was very strange without you to help celebrate. I thought of you all day long. I miss you. At church yesterday, when they started to play "And I Will Raise Them Up," I started crying and couldn't stop.

Three years after Trena's death—

I miss you so much. My life has totally changed. I don't have a lot of motivation. I am on antidepressants, but I don't think they work well. I remember just a week before you died, Daddy told me you didn't want us to go to Parents' Day at school. I wanted to see you so badly. I had a beautiful butterfly on a chain to give you on your sixteenth birthday. I never saw you again.

I remember hearing your voice for the last time. I asked if you got the birthday package I sent you, and you said, "Yes, thank you." My last words on the phone that day were, "I love you."

You said, "I love you, too, Mama."

Red Roses for His Birthday

"It's a boy!"

The tears of two dozen relatives crowded into the waiting room of a small West Texas hospital greeted that announcement. The entire extended family was there for most of Kimberly Hargrove's seventy-two hour labor.

The new mother's pregnancy was nothing short of a miracle. Scarring from endometriosis left her with four miscarriages and little hope of having a baby. But a determined first child was finally born on August 31.

Christopher Joel Pereida left the world exactly twenty years later. He hung himself from an old oak tree just one block from his younger sister's home. Sitting under that tree from midnight until dawn, the high school honor student watched his only sibling walk by for hours, looking for him. He did not answer Marci's calls. He just sat there until the sun came up, tying small pieces of rope together until the length suited him.

Chris sat alone in the grass on that hot summer night. The day before, he sat in a crowded classroom preparing for medical school. He loved children and wanted someday to be a pediatrician.

But someday would never come. In the wrong place at the wrong time, Chris was arrested for drug possession, although it has now been proven the drugs were not his. Still, he was threatened into taking the fall for a drug dealer. Chris believed his only choices were to take the rap or lose his life.

That was just one event in a series of choices and challenges for Chris. He never quite healed from other life-altering experiences. His parents' divorce was the first. His sense of self and stability came from the two people he loved the most. A piece of his heart went with each of them when they separated.

The rest of Chris's heart broke when he saw his grandfather take his last breath. Grandpa Les suffered a massive heart attack, and Chris watched paramedics try to pound life back into him. His grandfather's eyes never opened again. Chris could only stand by helplessly as his best friend and confidant died.

On top of the normal struggles faced by adolescents, Chris also tried to live up to some sort of peer- and self-imposed image. Friends at school saw him as popular and funny, the king of fast computers and fast cars. He was all of that to others—none of that to himself.

He thought of those things as he sat behind bars. Scared and alone, Chris had no sense of identity, no sense of worth, no sense of who he was or where he belonged. He called his mother before being released. After a short conversation, with no indication to Kimberly that anything other than the obvious was wrong, mother and son said good-bye. Kimberly hung up, thinking everything could somehow be worked out.

Before walking to the oak tree later that night, Chris spent time with his sister. But Marci could feel a difference in her brother. He was no longer loving and attentive; he was cold and quiet.

At the stroke of midnight, he walked out of Marci's front door. When the clock struck three and Chris had still not come back, Marci called their mother. Kimberly held the phone tightly and felt as though she had been punched in the stomach. Something was terribly wrong. Just a few hours later, Lubbock police stood on her doorstep and proved that a mother's instincts never lie.

Losing her only son has taken Kimberly close to death. She now relies on medication to make it through each tear-filled day. But she has never cried more tears than she did the day she gave her baby boy his last birthday gift. She had planned to place the twenty red roses in his arms; instead, she laid them on his casket.

Christopher Joel Pereida
Twenty years old

My Dear Chris,

I still cannot believe that you are gone. I love you so much, and I don't know how I will go on without you. I fought so hard to give you life, Chris, and I don't understand why, exactly twenty years later, you decided to end that. My heart aches so much sometimes that I can't breathe.

I thought losing my daddy would be the hardest thing I ever faced in my life. I was so wrong. Losing you, my firstborn and only son, has simply devastated me. There are so many "whys" and "what ifs." If only I could hold you one more time and tell you just how much you mean to me.

I no longer fear death, because now I have just as much reason to go to heaven as to live on this earth. I pray that you will hear me when I talk to you. I talk to you almost constantly.

I pray that you know just how much you are loved and missed by everyone. I pray that you are with Grandpa Les now, and that you are both at peace. God only knows the pain you were both in while you were alive. The Lord will light your way now, baby. On that you can depend. You will live in my heart forever. Always remember that if nothing else is certain in this world, your mom loves you more than life itself. I love you, Chris.

Love,

Mom

Phoenix Rising

Around ten o'clock one November evening, Marge's water broke. Like his brother and sisters before him, this baby would be born at home. We spent the rest of the evening finishing our preparations for the birth of our newest child. But all too soon, the night turned into morning, and with no labor pains beginning, I called the doctor.

After a careful examination, the doctor told us with a smile, "Take her home and give her an enema. If labor doesn't start by this evening, call me."

We did just that, and Marge's labor progressed naturally. Our son, Nathan, was born on a bed set up in front of the wood stove in the living room. While he lay on his mother's chest, I cut the umbilical cord. So began his life separate from his mother.

This strong, healthy baby grew to be a loving and happy young man. Nathan had a love of trucks and heavy, earth-moving equipment. When he was nineteen, I co-signed a loan for his Ford New Holland backhoe. Ah, the day that was delivered! He was so excited. It was brought out to the house on a flatbed truck, all shiny and new, sunshine yellow, smelling like a new car. With a huge grin, Nathan started off down the road.

I have many such memories of my beautiful son. Each is a jewel I take out, look at, laugh over, cry over, and then gently wrap in the velvet of my mind for safekeeping.

I was at work the day Nathan died. At a little past eight in the morning, Marge's voice on the other end of the line said, "Nathan's dead. He hung himself."

"No, not my Nathan!"

Just allowing that memory to play through my mind puts me in such a dark, confining place. We had no warning, no idea that our son was contemplating taking his life. It's like driving through an intersection on a beautiful warm day and having someone run a red light in a Mac truck and broadside you. It rips your life to shreds in less than a heartbeat. Nothing can prepare you for the death of your child.

When we lost our baby girl, Rachel, I thought I knew what it meant to lose a child. How naive I was. With Nathan came twenty-two years of memories, holidays, and birthdays. I had my daughter for only two weeks, and yet, almost twenty-five years later, I still cry at the memories of her short life.

Such is the love that parents hold for their children. All of my memories have pain attached to them now. Only a parent who has lost a child can truly understand the bone-crushing ache that you go to sleep with at night and wake to in the morning. Truly, only a whisper-thin cord keeps us here on earth rather than following our children to wherever they have gone.

I find myself going to places where Nate and I spent time together—stores and movie theaters. It's as if I'm looking for him in some weird way, hoping against reality that I will see him at one of those places.

Nathan is buried on our property next to his sister. Therein lies another story, another memory. Rachel was originally buried at a different location, but that property was being sold, and we wanted to move her to the new farm with us. Twenty years to the day after we buried her, I asked Nathan and his sister, Becky, if they would help me move Rachel.

On a beautiful, clear August day, we walked to the top of the ridge on our new property, where there is a panoramic view of the surrounding Blue Ridge Mountains. One ridge after another disappears into the distant west. Nathan began digging a grave with his backhoe but ran into some really tough rock. We moved over to the left several feet and began again.

When he had finished, I said to him, "Don't forget now, when my time comes, be sure to dig to the left of Rachel; otherwise, you will be into that rock on the right."

Little did I know that in a few short years, I would be digging his grave to the left. Our son's suicide was such a shock. Nathan never appeared depressed, unhappy, or emotionally unstable. He was a levelheaded young man who had every reason to live and no reason to die.

About a year after his death, I read a magazine article about a prescription medication for acne, called Accutane. I recalled that my son had been on a medication for his acne, which at one time had been quite bad. I contacted my insurance company, and to my horror, found that Nathan had indeed been on this medication for at least six months at the maximum dosage possible.

The side effects of Accutane range from simple dry skin to birth defects. According to the FDA, Accutane can cause sleeplessness, feelings of unhappiness, suicidal thoughts, aggressive behavior, and even suicide itself. At the time our son was taking Accutane, he was twenty, so we were not required to give our permission. Also, at that time, the health warnings had not listed psychotic behavior as a side effect.

As our children grow up, we have milestones to mark the passing years—their first steps, their first haircuts, their first solo rides on bikes, the day they get their driver's licenses, the day they marry. Our milestones for Nathan are now of a different nature: the day we brought his headstone to the cemetery, the day the name plaque was installed, the way the new grass is growing over his grave. Not monumental milestones, such as a grandchild being born, but milestones nonetheless.

Suicide is not a solitary act. When my son died on that mountaintop, a part of me died with him. I never thought it was possible to miss another human being as much as I miss that boy. I hope with all my heart and soul that by passing some of his pain to me when he died, he found the peace and serenity that eluded him while here on earth.

Willis Day
Nathan's Dad

Willis Day has filed a lawsuit against the manufacturer of Accutane.

Nathan Samuel Day
Twenty-two years old

Nathan's father wrote this letter the day after Nathan died.

> Dearest Nate,
>
> I'm sitting here in front of the computer trying to write something to you, but I don't know what. When you took your life, you took part of mine. I love you so much! I wish I had said that while you could still hear. I wish you had been able to talk to me, to come to me, but I know we didn't share things that way. I kept my feelings inside, embarrassed to say how I felt, always regretting the things I didn't say to you and your brother and sisters.
>
> I would trade places with you without hesitation. I have had most of my life, but you had all of yours yet to come. I could ask you why until the day I join you, but silence is all that I'll hear.
>
> I don't know what to say, Nate. I miss you so badly that I can hardly think. If I live another thirty years, the pain I feel this morning will still be with me.

A part of me keeps thinking that I will wake up from a bad dream—that you are sound asleep in your bed or chatting on your computer, and that these past twenty-four hours will fade, as all bad dreams do.

Your mom is in such pain that I don't think it will ever end for her. You were the light of her life, her right arm, her greatest helper. She, like me, never showed her feelings, but you know now that she loved you so very deeply.

I hope you are standing over my shoulder, reading this as I write. I don't know if such things are so, but I like to think they are. You were not much for the esoteric, or religion in general. I guess you know a little better now what lies after life on earth.

Robert and I went up to Poor Mountain yesterday afternoon to get your truck, but the police had driven it away. We found the mud holes from the directions you left me. I think we found the spot where you had parked.

It's now 6:00 a.m., twenty-four hours since you left—but you will never leave my heart. I love you so very much.

Dad

Wednesday's Child

"Wednesday's Child" is full of woe. That child sees the injustice and unfairness in the world. That child is the one who will make a difference.

Rain was falling the Wednesday morning Buffy was born. A classic California beach baby, she had blonde hair, hazel eyes, a blinding smile, and a magnetic personality. Her mother knew this child would be special. She had God-given great looks and a beautiful spirit. That spirit was a lighthouse, guiding others safely through crashing waves, keeping them away from sharp rocks on the shore.

Buffy was adventurous and open-minded, playful and carefree. She was a fashion model in high school, but made sure she was more than a two-dimensional color glossy. While still a teen, she moved out of her mother's home, ready to take on the world.

To describe her would be, in the best of all ways, to call her a newborn colt—ready to run wild, but not quite able to because its legs aren't strong enough. Seeing that colt finally run is a magical sight, just like Buffy was.

As elegant as she was, she also had a clumsy side. An excellent downhill skier, she would trip getting off the lift. She could cut across the wake behind a ski boat, but would slip getting out of the boat to put her skies on.

Those quirky qualities would embarrass most people, but Buffy would just toss her head back and laugh. A skinned knee, a raw elbow, a bruised leg—it didn't matter. Nothing was going to keep this colt from running.

She had an appreciation for the finer things in life, evident in her professional position at a five-star restaurant. Buffy started as a hostess, and to no one's surprise, worked her way up to banquet manager.

But the woman with the heart of gold and soul of serenity, the woman who danced with the wind and sang with the birds, had her own private war. She began battling depression about three years before her death.

She was twenty-nine when she drove her car off a 300-foot Palos Verdes cliff. No longer able to guide others safely home, she was the one now crashing on the rocks. The lighthouse that had shone so brightly for so many could no longer shine for itself.

Buffy left this world on a foggy Wednesday. She leaves behind so many who loved her, who are filled with warmth when they remember her smile. This "Wednesday's Child" really did make a difference.

Buffy Leigh Bergsetter
Twenty-nine years old

Dear Buffy,

If I could turn back time, I would spend just one last day with you. I would show you how many people loved you. I'd take you to all the places you loved and show you all the beautiful things you enjoyed. I would spend your last night with you whispering in your ear how important you are in my life. I would hold you in my arms, kiss your tears away, and never let you go.

Our lives have forever changed since you left us. Things just aren't as good as they were when you were with us. You brought joy into all of our lives. We will always have an empty chair at the table now.

I would like to talk to you, my sweet baby girl, about the note you left. You told us you were sorry. We are sorry for how much pain you were experiencing. To have taken such drastic action, you must have been in unbearable pain. I wish life had been kinder to you, my darling girl. You said we should go on without you. Tell me how I'm supposed to live without you. I try to breathe, to put one foot in front of the other, and to continue living, but I don't feel much anymore.

I also doubt my parenting skills. I can't offer advice to your sister or brother anymore. I gave you so much of what I had and the result was, well, you know. How can I ever feel comfortable trying to help them solve their problems, when I failed so miserably with you?

I wear your clothes now; can you imagine? I have two overflowing closets. I can't let go of any of your things. I do anything I can to feel close to you. Your room still has your scent.

In the morning when I get ready for work, I remember our last hug. I hope I never forget. You told me you would get through that one day for me. What happened? I have tried to retrace your steps, only to come up with more and more questions. I'm haunted by the questions.

I pray every night that I will dream of you, and most nights I do. I love to sleep now. But there are so many things I can't do anymore. We were always going to help each other get through this life—what did I do wrong, Buffy? How did I let you down?

I hope you found peace and you are in a good, happy place. Please don't ever forget how much I love you. Until we are reunited, I will try my best to carry on. I know you were counting on me to be strong. Dance with the angels, my sweet daughter. Be forever joyful, and please be there to meet me when my time comes.

All my love always,

Mom

Homemade Heart

How does one commemorate the life of a special son? I tried to think of how to explain the many feelings I have had since Keith died. But how does a mother share how blessed she was to have had Keith as a son? How does a mother show how proud she was of her son without sounding too boastful? How does a mother tell you about a son who always lived on the edge of mischief—one whose laughter lit up a room?

How does a mother talk about a son who was always the big brother to his sisters, or pass on the special ways he touched his grandparents' lives? But most of all, where does a mother find the words to describe the twinkle that was always in his eyes?

Memories are all we have left of Keith, but what great memories. I would like to share one of my favorite ones with you. On Valentine's Day, when Keith was five years old, he had forgotten the day was important to me. I gently reminded him that I didn't get a Valentine from my special son. Keith just smiled and said, "Wait just a minute, Mom."

He ran up the stairs, and within minutes, a Valentine's Day card was in my hands. The card was a simple red heart, and it read, "Happy Valentine's Day, Mommy." Inside Keith wrote: "Roses are red, violets are blue, I have no money, so I made a card for you."

Yes, each day we will miss Keith, but please know that by talking about him, you keep his memory alive. Please say his name, and be sure to have a twinkle in your eye.

Carol Loehr
Keith's Mom

Keith Richard Loehr
Twenty-nine years old

Dear Keith,

Every day I miss you more. You were my firstborn, and all I can do is think back on the wonderful times I had being your mother. When you were a baby, still in your crib, you would wake up around three or four every morning, happy to start your day.

I was so tired, but I would go into your room and talk to you. With your big smile, how could I resist your excitement of a new day? I would take you downstairs, and we would play. The only problem was that it became a bad habit.

The doctor told me that to break the pattern I would have to let you cry in your crib. I lay in bed with Dad and cried, too. The pattern was broken, but I am not really sure who won.

I can remember your love for my mom, Grandma Ilijanich. At her funeral service you knelt by her coffin, talking to her. You were such a wonderful grandson. You called Grandpa Ilijanich when he was so sick. You stood at his funeral mass, giving his eulogy. I was so proud of the young man you became.

One of the things I learned through your short, but meaningful, life was that you had such love for your family and friends. I never heard one cruel thing from you about your friends or family. You were always so understanding.

I now see the world through a different set of eyes. I take more time to look at nature and to listen to what people say. My life will never be the same, because you are no longer with me. I would do anything to have you back again, but since I can't, I will continue to bless the time I had with you.

My son, Keith, I will try to go on with you looking over my shoulder. I know you are in God's hands. Stay close in my heart until we meet again someday. I send you my love, now and forever.

Love always,

Your mom

The next story is also about Keith. It was written by his father.

Undaunted Courage

I am Keith's dad. Nearly three years have passed since he died. Perhaps you are reading this because your life has been impacted by Keith's death or by another suicide. I hope you can learn something from me.

We now know my son was depressed. Suicide is almost always the result of depression. The concerns, anxieties, and setbacks of life sometimes pile up so swiftly that a person is no longer able to cope. At some point in this downward spiral, the brain chemistry changes. The person does not feel right or think rationally.

Depression is an illness. Cancer is also an illness. We do not say people commit cancer. We should not say people commit suicide. People die of suicide because they are suffering from depression, a mental illness.

Keith was twenty-nine, active socially, and had dozens of friends. An avid fly-fisherman, he loved the outdoors. He participated in sports and adventures that often pushed him to the limits—backpacking into the Grand Canyon, downhill skiing on expert runs, rowing crew at UCLA, playing ice hockey, skydiving, scuba diving, and long-distance running.

After completing his MBA, Keith relocated to a new city and started a high-pressure job. Within six months, he was dead. No one understood the extent of his anxiety over his assignments. Given little direction, he had responsibilities he was not qualified to carry out. He was quite unhappy, and spent his last weeks vacillating between approaching outside recruiters and cramming by reading technical books late into the night.

Keith had never before exhibited signs of depression or any other mental disorder. After six months on this new job, however, he was losing sleep and losing weight. He covered up his anxieties so he would not alarm his friends. No one realized the danger he was in. Finally, having exhausted his physical and emotional resources, he was defenseless.

Job pressures and life stresses are something we can all relate to. But another piece of the puzzle of Keith's suicide corresponds to his love of adventure. A great possibility exists that certain people not only enjoy these bold activities, but almost require them. We know that physical exertion can produce chemical changes in the body. These changes can create feelings of well-being, and at their limits, euphoria. Certain people's brain chemistries may actually require a push to extreme limits to achieve what normal people feel at lesser levels of exertion and risk.

I recently read a book about the life of Merriweather Lewis, one of the most renowned US explorers. Imagine my shock when I read about his success as an explorer, his friendship with Thomas Jefferson, his frustration as a government bureaucrat, his struggles to complete a project, and his suicide. Thomas Jefferson described Lewis as having undaunted courage; those are the words I hold in my heart about Keith.

As I have worked to understand Keith, I have gained a deeper appreciation for the beauty and balance found in nature. Keith, with his courage and love of adventure, is in the company of many great men and women. These people tested themselves with some of the greatest experiences this planet can offer.

In his short life, Keith experienced things many of us will never try, even though our lives may be two or three times as long as his. I have developed a deep admiration for his accomplishments, a compassion for his struggles, and a gratitude for the blessings that his life brought to mine.

Dick Loehr
Keith's Father

Keith Richard Loehr
Twenty-nine years old

Dear Keith,

I recently went into your apartment for the first time. I apologize for not visiting you after your move to Minneapolis. I think my priorities were wrong. Sorry. As a consultant, I sort through this by thinking about phase number one. For me, phase number one is driving my car, listening to the Sarah McLachlan CD *Surfacing*, and starting with track number two ("I Love You"). For anyone who has lost someone, this is a good place to start. I cry a lot. It is supposed to be good for me. How will I know when this phase is over?

When I get sad, I say a prayer and think about all the wonderful memories. You would like that. You were a beautiful person, touching so many lives in such positive ways. Letters are pouring in from people I have never met. They help me know you better.

The good memories are plentiful. Your hockey team when you were six years old. Hockey practice at 6:00 a.m. at North Park. Geese flying overhead in the sunrise. You, Cindy, and Carrie on the beach—our favorite family vacations! You, as a young adult, making the UCLA crew team. And me, making the coaches upset by showing up after practice with a trunk full of orange juice and doughnuts.

And our father-son salmon fishing adventure at the Iguigig Lodge. I sat by the floatplane, admiring your spirit as you waded far out into the river, pursuing your dream. For a rookie fly-fisherman, I did catch some pretty decent salmon, right? At the end of the week, I suggested that we do it again.

Your reply was, "Sure, but you need to work on your fly-fishing technique." I might just do that, Keith! I miss you terribly, but I have so many wonderful memories.

Love,

Dad

Ray of Sunshine

Raymond Webb was a happy little boy. Happy, that is, until he was three years old. That's when he heard me screaming in our front yard. That's when he found out that his father had put a gun to his own head and pulled the trigger. That memory stayed with Ray forever. A widow at only twenty-one, I did my best to raise Ray, his brother, and his sister.

Ray grew close to his grandfather in the months after his dad's death. Grandpa had horses, so Ray spent most of his days riding and playing cowboys. That's also when Ray learned that his grandmother took her life just five years earlier.

Despite our family's traumatic past, Ray was well-adjusted and heading for a bright future. His grades were good, and he was popular in school. But when Ray was fifteen, that bright light began to dim. His stepfather and I were divorcing, and things just didn't seem so happy anymore.

Ray got hooked on methamphetamines. He tried to stay away from drugs; they just kept calling him back. But he did try. He got married and had two beautiful babies. Still, the drugs pulled him back in, and that made Ray angry. The angrier he got, the more he self-medicated. It was a vicious cycle.

The combination of his temper and his taste for drugs eventually landed Ray in jail for almost a year. That's when he got tough. The jail time and rehabilitation seemed to be just what he needed. When he finally came home to his wife and children, he was clean and ready for a new beginning. But that beginning wasn't easy. Ray was fighting financial battles and addictions that he felt he could no longer beat. He lost the war soon after his release from jail.

He hung himself in a backyard garden gazebo. Did he get the idea from his dad and my mom? I don't know. What I do know is that my life has been completely ruined since my son's death. From the minute I found out, I felt like this would be it. I would never go back to being myself again.

It's been a nightmare. I go back and forth between finding my mom hanging in the garage, hearing from a cop that my husband, Tony, shot himself, and finding out about Ray. My mom's grave is too far away to visit, but I go daily to see Tony and Ray. How I miss them.

I never thought I would have to go through this again. I feel like my insides have been hollowed out. I have panic attacks. I can't sleep. I bite my lip until it bleeds. I have turned so gray that I don't even look like myself anymore.

My son was so giving and loving. I know he would have never left his family out of spite. He thought he was doing everyone a favor. He did not want to cause us any more pain. If he only knew he caused us eternal pain.

I have cried rivers for my son, his dad, and my mom. I used to want to live a long life, but not now. I could care less what happens to me. My only hope is knowing I will see them all again one day.

Linda Marquez
Ray's Mother

Raymond A. Webb
Twenty-five years old

My Dear Raymond,

I love you so very much. I guess you know that now. I feel so guilty, so ashamed, that I didn't see your unhappiness. I tried to make you feel better when I talked to you. How could I, as your mother, not pick up on what you were really feeling? I just don't know how I will go on without you. I have been trying to get better, but it is so hard.

I have started running again, but I find myself looking up at the sky, screaming, "Where are you? How could you just leave us like that? How am I supposed to go on?"

I want so badly to be with you, but I can't leave Sarah and Rachael. They are so young, and they are your kids, Ray. I know you weren't thinking about all of this when you put that rope around your neck. Still, I am left to put the pieces back together.

Ray, when they lowered your body into the grave, I wanted to scream for them to save room for me. I have never felt such agonizing pain. It still cuts through me.

I want you to be the first person I see in heaven. I want to see your sweet face and huge smile. I pray for you every day and night. Do you feel the prayers? I will see you when God takes me home. It is a day I am excited for. I used to be afraid to die, but not anymore. I feel guilty saying it, but I am looking forward to it. Please, please know that I love you.

Your loving mother,

Linda

You can find Linda's stories about mother and husband in "Children Left Behind" and "Loves Left Behind."

Chocolate Kisses

I was only twenty-one, and I was scared to death. My first baby was about to be born. Her dad, David, took me to the hospital, where nurses made me walk and walk, until I refused to walk anymore. David caught hell from me because he got me pregnant, and I was miserable. I was going to make him miserable, too.

About ten hours later, I went into full labor, and at 12:29 on a Wednesday afternoon, Susan Elizabeth Jones made her entrance into this world. She was the most beautiful baby I had ever seen—eight pounds, two ounces, thick dark hair, and a healthy cry.

So many memories of my little girl are kept close to my heart. When Susan was just four days old, David's parents came from West Virginia to meet her. David and I went out while they baby-sat. When we returned, Susan's grandpa was feeding her chocolate. It was the funniest thing I had ever seen. She was sucking away like someone was going to steal it from her. All her life Susan absolutely loved chocolate. Her grandpa did that to her. He is now in heaven, too, and I know they are laughing together.

Susan's father and I broke up when she was young. I then went through an awful marriage. Susan saw me physically and emotionally abused by that man and others—something her young mind could never erase. I finally found the strength to break out on my own. Susan and I both were growing and exploring. For her, that meant getting to know her biological father, someone she had not spoken to in years. But Susan felt abandoned again by her father when she found out David had a new family.

In middle school, she began to change. She quit liking school, started hanging out with the wrong crowd, and began smoking and drinking. I did all that stuff, too, rebelling against my parents. So I handled her like my parents handled me. I grounded her, whipped her butt, and talked to her until I was blue in the face.

Susan always cared about others—ironic, since she didn't seem to care about herself. She began cutting her arms and scratching names into her skin. The scars! I was stunned to discover what she was doing. I was scared, and I didn't understand. We went to hospital after hospital until we finally found a counselor with whom she could bond. I thought we were making progress.

One night she came into my room and stretched out on my bed. We talked for a really long time, about everything and nothing. It was the best conversation we ever had. I was falling asleep, so Susan got up to go to her room. I remember her walking out the door like it was yesterday. I've wished a thousand times that I had called her back to tell her I love her, to hug her, to kiss her. But I didn't. I will live with that regret forever. It was the last time I saw my child alive.

The next morning I didn't bother to get Susan up for school. Knowing she wasn't going to go anyway, I avoided the confrontation. At lunch, I called home to see what was going on, and my boyfriend, Billy, answered. He said Susan was still sleeping. Well, that was unacceptable. She wasn't in school, so she should at least be doing her chores. He got her on the phone and I screamed at her. I told her to get her priorities in order, and I hung up.

That afternoon, Susan called me at work and asked me if I needed her to pick up her brother from school. I told her "No," that I took care of my priorities. That would be the last time I spoke to my daughter.

When I got home from work I sat down at the kitchen table and started going through the mail. Billy was standing inside the door, and to this day,

I swear I saw Susan sitting in the chair behind him. Billy then went to talk to a neighbor and about ten minutes later, came racing into the house.

He called 911 and screamed into the phone that Susan was hurt. The look on his face was terrifying. He ran back outside. I followed him into the woods behind our house. I didn't see her at first. Billy told the 911 operator that Susan was "hurt," not "dead." I was looking for blood. Then I saw her lying on the ground.

Neighbors were trying to do CPR. She wasn't breathing. My God, what was happening? No, this was not happening. Her eyes were closed, and she looked like she was sleeping.

"Susan, please wake up. I'm so sorry!"

My baby wouldn't wake up again. I saw her neck and knew my daughter was not with me. But my brain was rejecting that thought. Susan was not dead. She had not hung herself. Hours passed before all the police left and took Susan to wherever they took her. The police told me that they had found a knife under her body.

I tried to rationalize why my baby wanted to die. I thought she had impulsively tried to hang herself, and brought the knife to cut herself down if it hurt too badly. For five months, I thought it was all an accident. Then the police gave me back the things they took from Susan's room the night she died. I went through the boxes with a friend.

We found her suicide letter, and, boy, did she have something to say. The letters had all the answers. My daughter's suicide was not an accident, and I didn't know Susan as well as I thought I did. My daughter hid so much of her real self from me. I learned more about her after she died than I knew while she was with me.

I am still learning. Everything my daughter ever felt, she wrote on paper. I learned that my daughter was an angry young woman. Susan was sick, and she believed she was beyond repair. She was tired of struggling so hard to be "normal." I would have taken every ounce of her pain. I would have died for her. Didn't she know that?

This is the first time I have had to deal with death, and it is my child's. How unnatural is that? I will never be the same person I was on March 13 at 5:00 p.m. That woman died along with her daughter. I know now how quickly your loved ones can be removed from your life and from this earth. But my daughter lives on in a different way. She lives on through me, and the more I share her story, the more I heal.

Kristi Valis
Susan's Mom

Susan Elizabeth Jones
Fifteen years old

Dear Susan,

This is a letter I have wanted to write for a long time, but I didn't know how. How do you write a letter to your child who is no longer on this earth to receive it? I don't even know where to begin. I guess I should tell you that our lives are not the same without you. Nothing will ever be the same.

I am so sorry for what I didn't see. Hindsight is very powerful, and so is guilt. The guilt I felt after you died almost destroyed me, Susan. But I have come to terms with your decision. I now understand that you did not do this to me. You did this to make your pain stop.

I don't think I told you often enough how very proud I was to be your mom. I took it all for granted, baby girl, and for that, I am so sorry. I thought you would always be here. The day you died was very emotional, and I want to apologize from the bottom of my broken heart. I am sorry, Susan, for not understanding that you were calling for help. I just did not know, baby. If I knew then what I know now, you would still be here.

I will not lie to you. Living without my child is the most difficult thing I have ever done. I never dreamed this could happen to us. I never thought suicide would happen to you. You were the one who always picked us up and wanted to make us smile when we were down. How blind I was.

Your father refuses to talk to me now. I don't know how he's doing. I think he blames me for not taking better care of you. He wasn't so great either, but he thinks I could have done better.

In my heart, I believe God gave you to me because he couldn't reach me any other way. He used you to make me see how selfish and ungrateful I was. I am not selfish and ungrateful anymore. I have learned compassion in the most painful way possible.

I am a different mother now—the one you deserved to have. The drugs are gone, the screaming is gone, and the hitting is gone. I finally broke that cycle of abuse. It stopped the day you died, baby girl. Your brothers will not experience what you did. I promise you that. We do things as a family now. We spend quality time together. My job is no longer the most important thing; my family is.

Please forgive me for not understanding. I was human, and I was blind. But I swear I loved you with all my heart. I still do. Sleep with the angels, baby girl. You are in my heart forever.

Mom

Survivors Road2Healing

The phone rang at about 10:30 on a Monday night. A hysterical woman on the other end demanded to know who I was. She then told me my only son had just shot himself. He was dead—dead at twenty-seven.

My world blurred into a ball of pain, confusion, denial, and shock. A mother isn't supposed to bury her children. Mothers have a way of knowing things about their kids. How could I have not known his desperation? Why didn't he think I could help?

Losing a child to suicide is often more than a mother can deal with. A mother is the nurturer, the protector. Even in the animal kingdom, the mother makes sure nothing hurts her offspring. How does a mother possibly regroup after such a loss?

I found myself struggling with the toughest decision of my life. I could give in to the pain or do everything in my power to save another mom from this intense agony. You see, in all things, we have choices. You can get bitter, or you can get better. I wasn't willing to become one of the living dead.

The first year was the toughest. I lived many days moment to moment and clung desperately to my Father, God. He has been faithful to me and helped me become founder of Survivors Road2Healing. I have an online support group as well, and the group has walked thousands through crisis days and nights to a place where they find healing is possible. This is my passion, because there was a time when survival was questionable. I'll never forget the pain, but I made it, and you will, too.

Let me introduce my loved ones: Robby and Markie. Robby, my son, was such a thinker, even when he was little. He loved racing his bikes and doing crafty things, like making kites all by himself. He also loved tomatoes fresh from the garden. He asked more questions than most people could ever come up with. We still have brownies and his favorite ice cream, mint chocolate-chip, to celebrate his birthday. We buried him the Saturday before Thanksgiving.

Rob was my firstborn and my only son. I called him "my boy Elroy," and I can't wait to see him again one day. Thank God this parting is only temporary. He isn't really dead. He has just moved to heaven.

Markie, my nephew, was the stinker, and all boy. The curious one, an investigator—he was never still. He had the most gorgeous eyes. I have never seen anyone with eyes that danced the way Mark's did. He was one of those kids who could irritate the fire out of you, and then be so entertaining that you wouldn't remember why you were mad.

Rob and Mark were two weeks apart in age, and inseparable. They were more like brothers than cousins. Mark was my "second son." It hurt just as badly as if he were my natural-born son, when at the age of twenty-three, he hung himself. Four years later, my Robby shot himself. The boys are buried side by side, with matching headstones. Now they are back together, laughing and cracking jokes.

Healing is a slow process, but please remember that it's just that—a process. It takes time to sort it all out. It's a long, hard road to learning how to separate yourself from the pain. You need to talk, vent, and even repeat yourself over and over again if necessary.

I urge you to read books that can help you understand what you feel. Don't try to lock it out, or your pain will show up later in health issues. And please, allow each member of the family to work through this in his or her own way. We all heal differently, and this is not a time to try to fit into someone else's box of "this is how it must be done."

God bless you, and remember, you can reclaim your life. Also remember that in the time it took for you to read this story, someone else suicided. Almost 40,000 suicides occur each year in the United States. There are more suicides than homicides in the US. We are not singled out. The pain we know is widespread. Reach out for help—please. It's there.

Louise Wirick
Rob's Mom and Mark's Aunt

Robby James Wirick
Twenty-seven years old

Dear Robby,

I never would have imagined the silly things that would remind me of you. Freshly mowed grass reminds me of when you were about ten, sniffing the air. Oh, how you loved to smell freshly mown hay. When the farmers down the street mowed, you would hop on your bike and head for the corner. You would just sit there taking in the smell that reminded you of Grandpa's farm.

There are so many times I wish I could just chat with you. I'm sure you know you have a nephew who just turned two. He looks just like you and even has part of your name. Do you remember how your oldest daughter looked so much like your sister, and how we laughed about it? How ironic that your sister's son would look just like you.

Remember how you wanted to learn to make Web pages? Well, my son, you now have several Web pages sporting your picture. You are seen by thousands. They are not the kind of Web sites I ever wanted to see you on, but they have touched many lives. You would be proud of that because you had such a big heart.

When I think of you, I see you and Markie exploring heaven, free from anger. I had no idea that anger and head trauma could be related. I am so sorry that I thought you just had a bad attitude. I had no idea, Rob.

I find great comfort in knowing you are with Jesus, and that this is a temporary separation. One day I will be there with you. Until then, I have "Survivors Road2Healing" to keep me busy.

Remember what you said when you were little? "Mommy, I love you great big, way up to the sky!" Well, my son, I love you great big, way up to the sky!

Until I see you again,

Mom

Robby's sister wrote him a letter that you can find in "Siblings Left Behind."

Hindsight

Ian decided to be born while much of the hospital staff was at lunch. No one listened to me when I said he was coming. I was told that I was making too much noise and to go back to bed. But from the beginning, Ian was not one to conform. He wanted to be born right then.

During the first two years of Ian's life, his cry was high-pitched and piercing. He would arch his back and cry as though in agony. The sedatives prescribed only stimulated him. I believe Ian suffered from cerebral irritation at birth. Minimal research suggests brain trauma may eventually contribute to suicidal behavior.

Sometimes after our loved ones die, we see only the good things and tend to paint them as saints. Well, Ian was no saint. We fought quite a lot, as did Ian and his younger brother, John, although they truly did love each other. Sometimes my only peace was when I went to the bathroom and locked the door. In hindsight, I should have unlocked the door.

I often felt Ian was vying for my attention and resented the fact that John got extra attention. John was hospitalized on a regular basis for severe asthma. I was scared he was going to die. I had a feeling one of my kids was going to die. I thought it would be John. Even though Ian kept many feelings to himself, he did tell me he couldn't understand the cruelty, pain, and wars in the world. He said he wished he had a magic wand to make it better.

Not settled at school, Ian would have benefited from home schooling. He was a victim of bullying. When he was thirteen and at boarding school for a year, a live-in housemaster physically abused him. He was dragged out of bed and held against a wall, where he was strapped.

When Ian was about sixteen, I encouraged him to live with his father, believing he would benefit from being with his dad. I missed Ian immensely. I found out after his death that he really missed his mum, too.

At seventeen, he fell deeply in love. A bit like Romeo and Juliet, they wanted to run away together. I talked them out of it and thought everything was okay. I just didn't realize the seriousness of things. Hindsight once again.

The girl's family tried to split the two up, and eventually, the girl was sent away. It broke Ian's heart. But he was further crushed when he received a letter from her saying she wanted to break it off for good. Later, we discovered her family had encouraged her to write the letter. Ian received the note the same week he died. Three days before Ian's death, his girlfriend discovered she was pregnant. Ian never knew.

That week was the school prom. Ian got in a fight with a group of teens who often harassed him, making fun of his short hair and of his membership in the Army Reserve. Several of them attacked Ian, kicking him to the ground.

Beat up and bruised, Ian wandered home in the dark. Very late that night, Ian's father thought he heard a door banging. He walked to the kitchen and saw Ian's light was still on, so he went to check on him.

Ian was on the floor. Thinking he had fallen asleep there, his dad went to get him up. That's when he saw the gun and the spent shell. As he turned his son over, Ian's head made a sloshing sound. His father told me he would never forget that sound.

Ian died from a self-inflicted gunshot wound to the brain, the shotgun placed in his mouth. Our struggle to survive has been endless. It changes with each second, minute, and day. Just when I feel I am going along quite well, something twists in my gut, and I feel the loss again.

My son, John, has been an incredible support, and I often wonder if I have been as much to him. Sometime after Ian's death, I asked John what I could have done to be a better mother so that Ian would still be alive. I was waiting to hear that I shouldn't have done shift work, moved around, traveled, or a host of other things.

John looked at me and said, "Mum, you are fine how you are. You didn't kill him."

Ian, like many other young people, is an example of the sensitivity, gentleness, and talent we need in this world. I do not believe he chose to die. He wanted to get rid of the pain that was destroying his soul.

I feel for him, more than I have ever felt for myself. To feel so devastated and see absolutely no hope, that must totally be the end. I believe he would want me to continue as best I can and do what good I can for others. This I will do, for Ian, John, myself, and all of you out there.

Marie-Clare De Vere
Ian's Mother

Ian James Miller-De Vere
Seventeen years old

To My Loving Son Ian,

I remember your love for animals and gentleness with them. As you smuggled them inside, thinking I didn't know, I would say with a smile, "What have you got this time?"

I also remember our clashes. We were too alike. I wouldn't let you or your brother leave the house without a hug, a kiss, and an, "I love you," no matter how angry we were with each other. I remember your amazing original drawings and homemade cards.

I am glad I told you I was proud of everything about you. I am glad I said I was sorry when I was cranky with you when it wasn't your fault. I am thankful I told you how talented, loving, good looking, clever, intelligent, and gifted you were. I don't regret anything I did—only the things I didn't do.

While admiring the beautiful sunrises and sunsets, I hear your voice echo, "Hey, Mum, look at that beautiful sunset." You really appreciated and respected the beauty and miracles of nature. I used to call you "the professor" because you were often collecting stuff to make something.

I will always carry with me the little card you gave me for my birthday when you were just a young boy. You wrote: "Happy Birthday, Darling, Wonderful, Amazing, Excellent, Fantastic, Mother. Love from Ian." To the side you added, "You will get something."

I wish I could get you back. I love you forever, Ian, and miss you so very much.

XXX

Absent without Leave

He wanted to travel the globe and fill his passport with exotic stamps from foreign countries—to grab the world in the palm of his hand and absorb everything outside his home in the Missouri Flatlands. Randy "Pete" Hecox was a country boy, a good-natured, sweet-talking, quiet young man with a wholesome heart and a gentle smile.

He was one of nine raised in a one-bathroom home by the firm, yet loving hand of his mother, Alice. Life was happy, but there was no denying it was hard. Money was tight; still, Alice made sure their home was filled with laughter and love.

As a child, Randy would squeeze up to the supper table with his poodle, Gipsy, by his feet. He would look around that crowded kitchen and dream of having a family of his own, a family with whom he could travel the world.

On his way to fulfilling that dream, he discovered deceit. He filed for divorce after finding out his wife was cheating on him. So he decided to see the world—alone.

Randy joined the army, where he found pride and honor in giving back to the country he loved so much. He fought in the Gulf War. But when he came back from overseas, he had changed. No longer the carefree, kindhearted boy his mother once knew, he was distant and depressed, angry and affected.

It wasn't until that fateful July day that Alice became painfully aware of how different he really was. Randy was headed out of town and asked his mother to take him to the airport. She knocked on his apartment door several times. Calling his name, she knocked louder. No answer. She opened the unlocked door and stepped inside. It was quiet. Peaceful.

Alice walked to his bedroom, still calling his name. She found him lying on an air mattress on the floor. She leaned down to wake him. Then she saw the blood, the gray color of his body, the gun. He wasn't sleeping at all.

She will never forget the sight or smell of that moment. Nor will she forget the feeling she had as she touched his body and asked God to forgive him. She felt a powerful, comforting presence in the room. She knew then that Randy was on another journey. This time to a place far beyond Missouri—far beyond any place either of them could imagine.

Randy Reed Hecox
Thirty years old

Dear Randy Pete,

Why did you have to go? If love could have kept you here, you never would have left us. A dark hole is in my heart. I feel so guilty for not being there for you. I would have died for you. Why couldn't you see that? I raised you all by myself— no easy job. So why do I feel I let you down?

I try not to be bitter, but who pays the bills left behind? I love and miss you so much. Will the tears ever dry up? I think I know why I was the one chosen to find you. You knew I would take care of you in death as I did in life. I do try to go on with life, but it's really hard with you gone.

I feel you near me sometimes. I thank God for the thirty years I had with you, but that was not nearly enough. You left a lot of heartache behind, but I know your pain and your wars were a lot worse than ours. I wish I could have done more for you. If only I had one more try at being a better mom.

If I had only known the outcome, I could have said good-bye. The grandpa you never got to know is lying right beside you at the cemetery. I never got to say good-bye to him either. I know you two are playing music and cards up there. My dad can now take care of his grandson. I am so proud of you. I love and miss you so much.

Please know, as I write this and pass it on, that you will always be a part of my life, day in and day out. I shall never forget you or stop talking about you. You will live in my heart for as long as I draw a breath in my body.

Love you, my little drummer boy,

Mom

The Purple Connection

Of all the joys and challenges that we experienced with our daughter, one stands out more than others. It ties together the past, present, and future.

When Rachel was a teenager, we faced many typical challenges. During one in particular, I had been away for a couple of weeks on a trip with my parents. Upon my return, I discovered that our daughter had dyed her hair purple! I was speechless. I had two choices: to accept her decision, or to be angry. I decided to have fun with it.

Her birthday was just days after that. I planned a surprise party for her. Guess what color the cake, the balloons, the flowers, and the rest of the decorations were? Purple!

Flash forward a year to the day since Rachel suicided. I'm standing at the front window. Cold weather left the trees bare, but something catches my eye in the front yard. It's a balloon in the brown branches of one of the trees. Care to guess the color? Rachel's favorite—purple! I know why it's there, and I am grateful for the message. Rachel will always be with us. Not even death can sever the bond of love.

Monika Marie Lewis
Rachel's Mother

Rachel Marie Lewis

Twenty-one years old

"I Can't Believe"

I can't believe I have to endure this pain, that I won't see you the rest of my life. I can't believe that of all the pain I've endured in my life, I must endure this, too.

I can't believe I'll never hug you again. Why did suicide have to come to our lives?

There is no end to the pain in this loss—only enduring. Some days are better than others. "Ich liebe dich."

Monika Marie Lewis

Rachel was diagnosed with schizophrenia when she was twenty. She learned the words "Ich liebe dich" when she was just a toddler. It means "I love you" in German and is engraved on a rock on Rachel's grave.

White Candlelight

A happy marriage, healthy children, a terrific job, and a beautiful home—it sounds great. To those who don't know me, my life is picture perfect. I have been married for two years to a wonderful man. Ric and I love our life together and the time we spend with our blended family—Shawn, Steven, Seth, Nick, and Sarah. But things are not always as they seem. All five of my children are not here with me. One of them now watches over us.

The day began as any other Saturday—a few errands, some shopping, and an appointment at the beauty salon. After my appointment I stopped by the apartment three of my sons shared to show off my new hairstyle.

Steven and I were catching up on family stuff when he told me Shawn had not shown up for work that morning, strange because Shawn never missed work. I thought maybe he and a friend were playing hooky. I laughed, thinking I would tease him later.

Seth then walked in, and I could tell that something was terribly wrong. He told us he found a suicide note, dated and signed by Shawn at 1:35 a.m. He also said the window screen in Shawn's bedroom had been pushed out from the inside, and that Shawn had apparently climbed out the window. Shawn's 9mm semiautomatic handgun was also gone.

I looked around his room for clues. Shawn could not have been serious about wanting to kill himself. I refused to even consider the possibility. I checked with his work to see if he had called, but he hadn't. My daughter hadn't heard from him either.

That's when I called the police. While we waited for them to arrive, Steven found Shawn's wallet with his identification and his gun permit. I prayed that the police had picked him up for carrying a weapon without a permit and that he was sitting in jail.

The police finally arrived, along with another man who asked all the questions. When he realized I was Shawn's mother, he asked if we could talk someplace private. He then introduced himself as the coroner investigator.

The word coroner never registered in my mind. He said a young man matching Shawn's description had been found on the lawn of a church—a church I used to belong to. The man was leaning against the church, beneath a large window shaped like a cross. He was holding a photo of himself and a girl. Only his keys and a dollar bill were in his pockets. That's when I found out my son was at the Lucas County Coroner's Office.

The realization that my precious son was dead hit me so hard I almost passed out. My ears heard the words, and my brain made the connection, but my heart refused to believe that my child, whom I had carried for nine months, could have done such a terrible thing to himself—or to me.

I couldn't stop touching everything in Shawn's room. I could feel his presence. I could smell his cologne. His open pack of cigarettes sat on his nightstand. Mail was scattered on his bed. There had to be a mistake. My son wasn't dead. Shawn was so full of life and had a good, steady job and a wonderful sense of humor. This just couldn't be happening.

But his heart had been broken by a woman—the same woman in the photo. It was too much for him to handle, and this was almost too much for me to handle.

Shawn's dad and I lit a white candle at his funeral to represent the life we gave him. Each of his siblings lit a blue candle from Shawn's light. My children and husband were my guiding light that day. Without them the path would have been too frightening. Shawn keeps his candle burning in heaven so I can one day find my way home to him. My life will then be picture perfect.

Kathleen (Kathy) Kay Braden
Shawn's Mother

Shawn Daniel Cook
Twenty-four years old

My Dearest Shawn,

Just three months have passed since you left me to be with the Lord, and I have finally collected my thoughts enough to be able to express them to you. A huge part of me ceased to exist when I was told you had died. I refused to accept that you chose a gun instead of life.

What were you thinking? Did you not care that your death would tear me apart? Was I not a good mother? When I left your apartment that day I wanted to leave you a note telling you that we would all be at my house. But you were already home, safe in heaven.

Oh, Shawn, how my heart broke when I stood on the other side of that glass looking at you. I begged God to let you sit up, but you just lay there so still under that white sheet pulled up to your chin. I wanted so much to touch your face, to gently kiss your cheek, to hold you in my arms. All I could do was stand there.

My emotions constantly change, so it's hard to function normally. I don't even recall what normal is anymore. You are the first thing I think of in the morning and the last thing I see at night. I wish I could pick up the phone and call you. We shared so much, my son, but you denied me the opportunity to reach out to you. Maybe I wouldn't have been able to help you, but now I will never know.

At first I blamed your girlfriend for your death. She stole you from me, accepted all your gifts, used you, cast you aside, and finally destroyed you. I will always blame her for that; but you made the decision to end your life. After reading your journal, I know that the pain and rejection you felt for so long just wore you down.

Please wait for me, Shawn. What a wonderful day it will be when I join you. I will hold you in my arms for eternity. Until then, when I feel a soft breeze brush my cheek, I will know that it is your gentle kiss, the reassurance that you are watching over me. As I touch the beautiful blue urn that holds your precious ashes, you will hear me say, "I love you, too, Shawn."

Love you forever,

Your mom

Shawn's fourteen-year-old brother also wrote a letter. You can find it in "Siblings Left Behind."

It's That Simple

Ben was so proud as he walked the high school hallway with his father. The two were alike in many ways—their laughs, their smiles, their sympathetic gazes. But with music, they were on opposite ends of the score.

Ben head-banged to heavy metal; his father, Don, jammed to jazz. But both took time to appreciate the other's tastes. That's why Don was at Ben's school that day. Ben volunteered at the student-run radio station and decided he and his father should play their tunes in their own "Battle of the Bands."

Don shared the sounds of Jelly Roll Morton and Fats Waller that afternoon, while Ben put the spotlight on Whitesnake and Black Sabbath. Father and son listened with open minds, but neither was swayed after their session. They did, however, walk away with a newfound respect for one another.

Don and Ben handled everything between them with open and honest communication. Countless numbers of teens and parents hit roadblocks, but not Don and Ben. They embraced their similarities and their differences.

Don and his wife, Karen, never expected to have more than one child. After Rebekah was born, Karen was diagnosed with cervical cancer, so it was music to their ears when they learned just four years later that she was pregnant again.

As much as he loved his daughter, Don wanted a son terribly. He knew this time that God would give him that son. Nine months later, Benjamin was born.

Don worked as a salesman, while Karen home schooled the children. However, once Ben hit his teenage years, he wanted to go to high school with the neighborhood boys. He did well at first and got involved with extracurricular activities. But Ben was a perfectionist, and putting so much stress on himself to succeed affected him physically and mentally.

After spending a year in public school, Ben couldn't handle it anymore and he burned out. He took time off from school the next year and focused on recuperating. He wanted to try again the following spring. Reluctantly, his parents agreed.

Don and Karen don't know exactly what happened to Ben at school, but they do know he was under pressure to perform. That pressure made him anxious and angry. They also know that only one week after returning to class, their sixteen-year-old son took his life.

There were no drugs, no girlfriend issues, and no history of depression. There were also no answers or explanations. Ben's note only asked them not to blame themselves, as, "This was inevitable. It's that simple."

Karen and Don tried to support each other, but with both of them in such pain, it was hard to heal their own hearts while being there for their daughter. Very little room was left for them as a couple.

Karen joined a support group, where she found strength, understanding, and compassion, but Don refused to have anything to do with a group. He could talk about Ben, but not about his death. Perhaps that denial led to what happened just a year and a half later. That's when Karen turned to a support group again, not because of Ben's suicide—because of Don's.

Benjamin Lowell Kimball
Sixteen years old

Karen began journaling one day after Ben died.

> Dear Ben,
>
> I love you! I wish you knew (and maybe you do) how many people this has affected. You never would have accepted it if we had told you how many people respected and loved you. My miracle baby, you grew into my perfect child.
>
> I was never disappointed in you—only astounded at the good, loving, talented person you were. You had so much potential. What could have troubled you so much that you couldn't talk to us? I can't imagine, and I guess I'll never know. I guess I'll spend the rest of my life trying to find the answer.
>
> What was the lesson for us, which sent you to us and took you away too soon? I will always search for the reason.

One year after Ben's death—

> I sit here alone at the edge of the sea and look off to the distant horizon, where the far edge of the sea blends with the edge of the sky, where they meet in a haze to create a special place filled with happiness and with peace. You are there in that special place.
>
> You are now a free spirit. But my silent, selfish wish is that those waves rolling in would carry you here even for a moment. I want you here at the edge of the sea, where it meets the edge of the sand, where I sit looking for you, so I could say, "I love you."

Two years after Ben's death—

I've made it through this second year without you. I've survived it, but just barely. There are more first-times of doing things without you as I begin to open myself up more to life. New meanings arise in old familiar things.

Especially difficult during this second year were graduation and your eighteenth birthday. I have survived, though sometimes I had my doubts. My memories are beginning to bring me solace.

Now I also have to work through your father's death. Following your example, which shattered him so, he took his own life, too—shocking, but not surprising to most. Others saw more clearly than I how much of him died with you.

I was so occupied with working through my own grief that I didn't see he couldn't work through his. I didn't see his deepening depression as I battled mine. Both of you have found your peace. How do I find mine?

You can find Karen's story about her husband in "Loves Left Behind."

Rainbows and Butterflies

I stayed home from work on the fourth anniversary of my daughter's death. My plans were a bit vague, except for the short trip I would make to Woodhaven Road, the place she picked to end her life. I needed to be there before 1:30, the estimated time of Arlyn's death. It had become a yearly ritual.

I went into her bedroom to get a few things to take with me that would remind me of her. I picked up a folder with some of the poems she had written. I also grabbed a framed photo of Arlyn when she was three years old. She was wearing a Raggedy Ann costume I had made. That made me smile. The room was full of Arlyn, but it seemed so empty. I closed the door. Time to go.

I put a lawn chair in the car, then slowly drove three miles to a place I hated, a place that held the most painful memory of my life. I parked the car next to a rickety wooden bridge that crossed a small stream. I stood alone on the dirt road and stared at the two handmade wooden crosses that announced Arlyn's death.

Sitting down, I realized I had placed the chair on the exact spot where my daughter's beautiful, healthy body had fallen. I briefly panicked and thought about moving, but didn't. Perhaps a morbid need to connect with her held me there. I opened the folder of poetic musings, and I read her words.

"The scent of death surrounds me, and I am overwhelmed by its beauty." Her hands had written those words, but her heart had felt them.

I looked up and stared at nothing in particular. It was terribly hot, much like the day Arlyn died. I glanced at my watch. It was almost that time. If her spirit were to arrive, it would be now.

I asked out loud, "How are you doing, Arlyn Darlin'? What's it like up there?"

No reply. I began to ask harder questions.

"Arlyn, do you miss us? When you pulled the trigger, did you have any idea of how badly your death would devastate your dad and me?"

Nothing. I had to try one more time. I would ask for a sign that she was here. I had waited four years. Long enough. I opened my eyes and searched for a sign. Then I realized I would not know a sign if I saw one. What did a sign look like? Was it blinking lights? A crash of thunder? What was I looking for?

Then I spotted yellow butterflies in the woods behind the crosses—pretty common in South Georgia this time of year. That was it!

I yelled, "Arlyn, if you hear me, will you send me a red butterfly to let me know you're okay? Will you send me a red butterfly if you know how much I love you and how badly I miss you? Please, Arlyn."

I closed my eyes and felt a cool breeze. I shivered. When I opened my eyes again, the yellow butterflies were gone. I sighed. Disappointed, I felt myself sinking. I was a reluctant traveler on this road. Sometimes it seemed too hard to go on. Sometimes I wanted to give up and join my daughter. I missed her so much.

A moment later, out of the corner of my eye, I spotted a red flicker by the stream. A large red butterfly came from under the bridge. Slowly it flew toward me, bobbing up and down. I held my breath as the butterfly got closer. The trees behind it faded out; all I could see through teary eyes was the red butterfly. It fluttered close to me, then flew all the way around the two crosses that bore Arlyn's name. I sat there so close I could almost touch it.

I have visited the place on Woodhaven Road many times, and the only butterflies I've seen there before were yellow. Was Arlyn letting me know she heard my cries and that she was at peace? Maybe she was letting me know she understood the depth of my love. Maybe she wanted me to know she was with me. I decided to take her gift of the red butterfly and reach out to others who grieve.

I started an online support group called Parents of Suicides. Today the group has members from around the world, an annual candlelight memorial, and a yearly retreat. We help each other deal with the issues unique to suicide, and we honor the memory of our sons and daughters.

I have also started the online support group called Friends and Families of Suicides. We are just beginning face-to-face support groups, with chapters in several states. I also have a group called Distant Drums, which serves Native Americans and Aboriginals who face very different needs when it comes to suicide. I wonder if Arlyn knows about her Cherokee ancestry.

I hope my daughter is proud of me. Even if she is, she could never be as proud as I am of her. It would make her smile to know that so many people all over the world have heard of her through my work. When she was little she dreamed of being Miss America. I think she has touched more people now than she would have if she had worn that crown.

Karyl Chastain-Beal
Arlyn's Mother

Arlyn Maria Beal
Eighteen years old

This is a journal entry Arlyn's mother wrote five months after Arlyn's death.

Dear Arlyn,

The day before your birthday, I debated whether to go to school, because I was feeling more emotional each day. But I went and almost made it. Around two o'clock, I could not hold back anymore, and I started crying. The kids are getting used to my tears now. I took them outside for a long recess. I stood alone and fought to regain self-control.

After school I decided to go to the cemetery. Your dad and I planned to go on Saturday, but I needed to go then and wanted to do it alone. When he is with me, I feel like I need to help him, and I cannot let go of my own emotions.

Rain fell fairly hard, but it did not matter. Some say rain is God's tears, but I am not sure if I believe in God anymore. I stood by your grave as the rain drenched me, and I talked to you. I don't know if you heard me or not. The visit was horrible. The excruciating pain I felt after you first died returned, and I wailed so loudly it frightened me. But I could not stop. The sounds emanated from my gut and seemed to be ripping my soul to shreds.

Driving home, I was amazed to see the most beautiful, perfect rainbow I have ever seen, arching itself across the highway as if I were driving through the center of it. I have always believed that a rainbow symbolizes hope. I could not help but read into that rainbow's great significance. I don't know what the hope is for, other than to be able to survive the rest of my life without you.

I went home, optimistic that your birthday would truly be a day on which we could celebrate your birth and life, rather than dwell on the terrible circumstances of your death. Before you died, Arlyn, death was simply a word I heard about. Not any more. Your death was the end of the world. I love you, my sweet little girl. You are the wind beneath my wings—forever.

Love,

Your mom

Help to Heal a Parent's Heart

For a parent to lose a child in any way is unthinkably painful. It is not supposed to happen. While we are never prepared to lose someone we love, a space in our consciousness exists for losing our grandparents, parents, and even siblings and friends. But we have no place in our consciousness to outlive our children.

Parents who have lost a child go through many of the same feelings one would feel with the loss of any loved one—shock, denial, fear, anger, resentment, despair, helplessness, and guilt. Those feelings are intensified for those who lose a child because, for many parents, a part of them feels like it died as well. All parents have hopes and dreams for their children. When that child dies, so do those hopes and dreams.

Suicide is an even greater tragedy because we think it is preventable. The "what ifs" and "if onlys" create deeper wounds (see "Garden of Angels"). Parents feel that they should have known; they should have been able to do something. Their duty as parents is to keep their children from harm. The parents' sense of utter failure just adds to the grief. Parents carry an added burden because they so often feel that the whole world thinks they failed.

A profound need exists to blame somebody or something when a loved one dies. It feels wrong to blame the person who has died, so we look elsewhere, anywhere else and to anyone else, including ourselves. You will see this blaming in many of the stories in this book. One mother wrote about her daughter's suicide: "The guilt I felt after you died almost destroyed me" (see "Chocolate Kisses"). Another parent puts blame on her son's girlfriend (see "White Candlelight").

Your children are always your children. You always feel the need to protect them and make everything all right. Most parents feel they should have known and should have been able to stop the suicide. But often, no one could have prevented it, not even the parents, just as they could not have saved their child from incurable brain cancer. It is as true for those who die from suicide as it is for those who die of brain cancer; they have suffered, and death is the only way they could see to end the suffering.

Grief, with all its similarities, is different for each person. Everyone has to deal with loss in his or her own way. It takes as long as it takes, and it is a wound that never completely heals. The pain becomes less intense as we move through the stages of grief, but it will always be there. If the feelings and emotions are not dealt with, they become like a bacteria that infects a wound. Trying to be "strong" just covers the wound and leaves it to fester.

Parents can do many things to move through the grief toward healing. The emotions that you feel must be acknowledged and accepted. Most importantly, hold on to whatever faith you can.

Gather family and friends together to talk about the one who is no longer with you. Talk about the wonderful and funny things your child did—the things that made you laugh, made you cry, and made you angry. Have everyone share stories about your child.

Another way to give movement to your emotions is to write. As soon as you can, write a letter to your child. Say what you would want to say right now. Writing not only helps us acknowledge and accept our feelings, it also helps cleanse the wound. Don't worry if you don't say everything you need to say. You may need to do this a number of times. Every release, however small, is a step in the right direction. There is a place in the back of this book where you can begin journaling.

To acknowledge and accept your emotions is a step in the direction of healing. Once you can do these things, release what you can. So much of our culture sees it as strength to keep all those emotions to ourselves. But what we hold back stays within us, festering. Gnawing away at us. The point is not only to acknowledge those feelings, but to express them.

Movement is vital. Linda wrote of beginning to run again, and as she ran, she would shake her fists at the sky and cry out (see "Ray of Sunshine"). This is a great step to help you heal. Don't be afraid of what you may look like or what people may say. Go somewhere you won't be seen if need be. Walk, run, turn circles. Give voice to your pain. Let the sounds be words or moans, wails or screams. It does not matter. Let go. You can only be free from your demons if you give them freedom.

As you heal, you can begin to find a way to help others deal with their loss. As you help them heal, you heal. You will never forget. The memory will always be sad, but the unrelenting and unbearable pain will ease. The stories "Survivors Road2Healing" and "Rainbows and Butterflies" both explore ways parents have made the choice to heal themselves by helping others.

The steps to peace are not easy, but they are simple. Forgive the one you lost, and forgive yourself. God speed you on your journey to peace.

Minister Charlotte Dunhill[1]

---

1. Charlotte Dunhill is Minister Emeritus at Christway Prayer Center in Arlington, Texas. Besides her one-on-one spiritual counseling, Dunhill conducts classes on "Happily Ever After: How to be a Loving Partner in a Loving Relationship."

Angel of My Heart
Siblings Left Behind

"Angel of My Heart"

I don't know where I belong
I don't know
But there's something that's burning deep in my soul
I believe it's you
I'm holding on to fate
And I'm longing for the moment to touch your face
I'm searching for the angel of my heart

—Tena Rae
From her song, "Angel of My Heart"
www.tenarae.net

Here's to You, Jude

This is how I remember you: at a table with friends, clutching a coffee cup, engaged in conversation, laughing. If ever a person loved a good story, it was you, Jude, especially when the story was about some absurdity of life.

Intelligence never impressed you, but quirkiness did. You were drawn to those who had a different take on things, although that alone was not enough. They also had to talk about their own humiliations and laugh until tears came to their eyes. You loved the ridiculous.

I'm still trying to puzzle out the last ten months of your life. I didn't know you were sick until Tracey called and blurted out, "Mark! I have terrible news. Judi just killed herself!"

Those words slammed me back with the feeling of instantaneous, crushing loss. Then everything fell into place. In fact, I did know you were sick, but you had so deftly steered me away from the truth that I came to believe it was a thyroid episode caused by wrong medication.

Beau called back in June; he sounded really shaken. "Mom has lung cancer."

A rush of adrenalized terror swept over me. I had anticipated this call as I watched you smoke and cough for years, but you had quit, and I thought the danger had passed. Now the horrible moment had arrived. My only thought was to race to your side and show you that if you were to die, it would be with us ringed around you, traveling that path as far as we could go, locked together as a family.

You, Tracey, and I had done much the same with Mom from the moment of her cancer diagnosis till her death. During the last eight months, each of us flew to Idaho Falls to be with her for two-week shifts. You knew we were well-versed in this routine, and you would see it begin the moment I walked through the door.

But your son called the next day with good news. Beau said it appeared you did not have cancer. You were suffering from dehydration. They had given you fluids, and now you were feeling so well they were releasing you from the hospital. The crisis was over.

I called you at home, and you sounded just great, laughing and bubbly about this whole hospital business. It was something to be brushed off as just another good story to tell in the future. You weren't quite sure what had happened, except that when you were reading e-mail, it began to look like Bulgarian. So you made your way to the hospital to discover you were dehydrated.

But you're feeling fine now, you said, and indeed, your voice sounded very strong. A bit too strong; I assumed you were just animated. Only later would I learn you were shouting through an oxygen mask. Even though you sounded well, my concern remained. I begged you to get a complete physical so you could assure yourself, and us, that everything was okay. I especially wanted you to get a chest x-ray. What did you think of such a silly request?

"Chest x-ray?" you might have said. "Oh, I've had my chest x-rayed, and that's why I'm sitting here at home tethered to an oxygen tank—waiting."

I called again the next day when Beau was there. You said you were eating like a horse and drinking gallons of fluid. The problem arose, you said, because the pharmacy had filled your thyroid prescription incorrectly. At last you had an answer to your dehydration and all the other strange symptoms that forced you to the hospital. Beau confirmed you were eating well and said you looked fine. My worries dwindled away.

It was all a ruse, though. Beau had rushed to Denver because he put two and two together and knew it was cancer, despite your protests. He confronted you. Although you were vociferous in your denials, he persisted till you acknowledged the truth. Cancer. Terminal. Then you swore him to secrecy. He was to tell no one. Not Tracey. Not me. Not Michelle. That was your wish—your demand. And he honored your wish, bearing this terrible knowledge alone, revealing nothing.

Three months later, you took everyone by surprise. Tracey said in an anguished voice, "Judi just killed herself!"

A friend once commented on how noble he thought suicide was. I disagreed, saying it depended on motive. Perhaps it's noble if the person does it out of some rational necessity or selfless reason, and if so, then I can easily honor you in that way. You didn't want to die. You said in your letters that you were greedy for more time, but you saw it wasn't to be. No amount of wishing would change that simple fact.

You crafted a remarkable ending for yourself. While you and I bantered harmlessly back and forth via e-mail, you were in and out of the hospital as your breathing became difficult and your other systems broke down. Occasionally your misery would show up in your messages, but I never caught on, because the next sentence would contain the easy patter about friends or weather.

Somewhere during this time, you finalized a local will, packed boxes of your things as gifts for friends, even called a local charity to come to pick up odds and ends. You wrote out detailed instructions: "No funeral! Cremation! Do with the remains what you want. The roof is relatively new, so don't worry about it. The small water damage on the wall was caused by something else. The new tile is for the upper bathroom. Either retile or sell it for $600." And you end with what is a wonderful statement about the simplicity of life and death: "The car has a new alternator."

Also during this time, you bought a gun.

As we arrived at your house, so fresh with the small necessities of daily activity, the clothes hanging in the closet, the clock ticking on the side table, we discovered that you had left each one of us a priceless jewel—a good-bye letter. The letters are remarkable in their tone. You don't want to die, but, there you have it. The choice is no longer yours to make. You recall the special moments, then you say what you want from us.

There is no hysteria, no angst, no philosophical wailing. The cadence of the sentences makes it all seem so natural, and in the end, the letters do their job. We stand up and salute.

With the completion of this final note to you, I push away from my desk and pour myself a glass of wine. Here's to you, Jude.

Mark Allen Brown
Judi's brother

Judi Hebert
Fifty-six years old

This is the letter Judi left for her brother, Mark.

Dear Mark,

Well, if Mother didn't tell you that you were a "good son," I will tell you that you have been a good brother. Sure, we've battled our way through, but I've always known that should I yell for help, you would be there, no questions asked. That has always been a comfort.

I think back, way back to Fifth Street, to our playing cowboys and Indians, your fires, our summers in Bakersfield—the best time of my childhood. Then the choices of my adult years— wondering about many of them, but sure that I wanted children, a home, a normal family situation. Well, I got part of it, anyway, plus a best friend in my own mother.

I am so sorry that things have to end this way. I yearn for more time to enjoy my family, to watch and see what happens, to laugh with you all. Have I ever told you that you have the best laugh I have ever heard? It always makes me laugh, too. It's such a real one.

Take care of my children. You have a new friend in Tess. Help her grow. She has lost many people in her life. And Beau, he is the best of me, were I bold enough to take any credit. Help Michelle, too. Time is short.

I love you and have never questioned your love for me. I have always known it.

Love, Judi

X X X X

Dial M for Mistake

My brother called moments after I walked in the door from our visit. Something had gone terribly wrong after I left his home. Allen said he had just shot and killed his wife. His voice was calm and clear, his tone decisive and determined. I couldn't even find my voice. I just stood there, not believing what I was hearing. He asked me to come over so that I could take care of his baby girl.

For my brother's sake, I tried to stay focused. I wanted to sit down and cry, scream, hit something, hit someone. Then came the questions. Should I call the police? Dawn's family? My family? I should have called them all. Instead, I grabbed the car keys and headed for the door.

I begged my husband to make the ten-minute drive with me, but he was too upset and refused to go. I wasn't afraid of Allen, I just didn't want to be alone, so my son stepped in to hold my hand.

When we got there, Allen came out on the porch, set his little girl, Taylor, down, looked me in the eyes, and then went back inside. I picked Taylor up and gave her to my son. I told him to take her far out in the yard and, no matter what happened, not to come inside. Then I went in behind Allen and shut the door.

He was standing in the middle of the living room with a cocked .38 in his mouth. I had tunnel vision. I couldn't tell what else was going on around me—if the television was on, if anyone else was in the room, if it was light or dark. All I could see was my brother with that gun. As I stood arm's length from him, he pulled the trigger.

I will never forget that deafening blast. Before the sound even stopped bouncing off the walls, Allen hit the floor. Somehow I managed to rush past his body and call 911.

It all happened so quickly, but what I saw is permanently etched in my mind. I went into my brother's bedroom after I hung up the phone. His wife, Dawn, lay dead on their bed. I couldn't think straight. So much blood. So much heartache. So much death. I will never know what really happened that night. All I know is that I loved my brother very much. He was my best friend.

Taylor was two-and-a-half years old when her daddy died. Her mother's parents have adopted her, and she is doing really well. She has red hair like her mama. She walks and talks just like her daddy. She was his pride and joy. I hope she will remember her parents as she gets older. With our help, I think she will.

My recovery from my brother's suicide has been long and painful. I struggle with it every day, suffering panic attacks when I'm awake and nightmares when I'm asleep. About a year after my brother died, I tried to kill myself by overdosing. Somehow I survived, but that, too, is a daily battle. I went to a psychiatric hospital for thirty-five days to get help.

Some people never get that help. I hope my story will aid someone who is contemplating suicide or surviving the loss of a loved one. If you are thinking about taking your life, please remember this: once it is done, you cannot undo it. There is help if you really want it.

If you have lost a loved one to suicide, I am sorry for your pain. But now is the time to heal yourself. Honor the memory of your loved one, but make your own future one day at a time. Thanks for reading my story.

Vickey B. Thomas
Allen's Sister

Allen T. Brantley
Thirty-two years old

Dear Allen,

Five years have passed since you died. It really doesn't seem that long since you were here and doing okay. I am not sure when it got to the point of not being okay. I thought you had a pretty happy home with your wife and little girl, but I guess it's not always as good as it looks. I know that you loved Taylor more than life itself.

I have tried many times to put myself in your shoes to figure out what happened. I tried to believe it was just an accident, but the sheriff said it wasn't. The investigation showed that you had apparently walked up to Dawn at the foot of the bed, held the gun about a foot from her chest, and shot her. No room for an accidental shooting.

What could have been said between the two of you that got so out of hand? When I left your house earlier that night, both of you seemed okay. Did I miss something? I know you tried to talk to me before I left, but you changed your mind. Was that it? I will never know now, and that haunts me. I am so sorry I couldn't save you or Dawn.

I am now trying to help other people who are traveling on this same road. The first stages of a suicide are so confusing, and since I have already been there, maybe I can help. It doesn't mean that I have forgotten you. It just means that I have to get on with my life. Suicide is not an option for me.

After all that has happened, I still love you as much as I did before you died. I have always been proud of you and proud to be your big sister. I want to make sure people know who you were, instead of only what you did. What happened in the end cannot be all there was to your life, even though I know it is all some people can see. I saw all the good in you and have those memories in my heart.

Taylor is so much like you it hurts. She has her mom's daintiness and your temperament. I hope she learns to control her temper better than you did. She seems to have adjusted to life without you and Dawn. Maybe it's because she was so young when you both died. Some day I guess she will come to me and want to know what happened. I will do my best to tell her, since I was there. I will see to it that she remembers you and her mom and knows how much she was loved.

I guess I should go now. I hope you know how much I love you and how much you meant to me. You will always be my little brother, and nothing will ever change that.

I love you,

Vickey

Red, White, and Bootsie

Prince Andy Gets Randy
The Prince and his Blonde Beauty
A Match Made in America

Oh, what the headlines could have read about Prince Andrew and the beauty beside him during his tours of Cape Canaveral. One of his US military bodyguards just happened to look more like Miss USA than a certified sharpshooter. The decorated naval intelligence officer could have won that crown if, besides beauty and brains, the qualifications included being an Uzi-handling special agent who went by the nickname "Bootsie."

Bootsie's mom was in a Mississippi hospital watching live coverage of that royal visit. She was not at all surprised to see her daughter standing guard next to the prince. What did surprise her, though, were the comments made by the media, speculating who the blonde might be.

"That blonde," Bootsie's mom smiled, "is my baby girl."

A lot of laughter followed Bootsie and her two sisters, Binky and Snooker, as they grew up. And not just because of their nicknames. They were known in their neighborhood as "Binky, Bootsie, and Snooker—the Three Sisters." Their parents called them by their real names only when the girls were in big trouble. Of course, that trouble was generally nothing more than prank phone calls, playing in the street, or pestering their brothers.

Bootsie's father was a naval pilot, a World War II veteran who had served on the staff at the Pentagon. That's where he met her mother, a secretary for the Joint Chiefs of Staff. Bootsie wanted to make her parents proud. An honor student, she believed in God, country, and family. As determined and iron-willed as her father, and as gentle and kind as her mother, she demanded nothing less than perfection. That rigid self-discipline helped her earn a prestigious career, but it may have kept her from accepting help when she needed it the most.

In the months before Bootsie's death, she became very depressed. She would only get out of bed to go to the bathroom. She wouldn't speak to anyone, not her husband, her two children, or her sisters. She had been suicidal for months, delusional and paranoid, so her mother-in-law moved in, and her husband took a leave of absence. Although her psychiatrist had her on a new medication, Bootsie was still under a 24/7 suicide watch.

But one morning Bootsie thrilled her mother-in-law and husband by getting up, taking a shower, getting dressed, and coming downstairs. She hadn't done those things in months.

She told them she felt better and was going to get a massage since she was stiff from lying around so much. Happy to see her acting more normal, they waved as she drove away, thinking the new medication was working.

Bootsie returned home quickly, claiming that the masseuse was booked. She told her husband she had stopped for gas and accidentally left the gas cap at the station. So he loaded their children and his mother into the car to go get it.

When they got home he ran upstairs to check on Bootsie. Then he realized she hadn't tried to get a massage. She had actually driven to a nearby town for a gun and some bullets.

No one knows why Bootsie ended her life. There was no note, so all their questions go unanswered. All her husband is sure of is that the God-fearing, military-minded, sweet-loving woman he fell in love with was his princess on the day they married. She will be his queen until the day he dies.

Diana "Bootsie" Lynn Santee Benson
Forty-three years old

Dear Bootsie,

I was out watering the yard early this morning before work. The sky was so blue it didn't look real. The sun warmed my face. The birds were singing and chirping, and the breeze was refreshing on my toes in the cool grass. I was smiling, just happy to be alive. How could you leave this?

You were so excited when you were pregnant with your first child. Do you remember how you played the sonogram video over and over, trying to show me why you knew the baby was a boy? And when he was born you made endless phone calls so I could hear him make all his baby noises. You had great pride in your son. How could you leave him? And your second child, your beautiful, gentle daughter, had your eyes. Your babies were everything to you. You loved them without reservation. How could you leave them?

How surprised I was the day I told you that you were my role model and that I admired you and wished I was like you. You admitted that I was your role model, whom you admired and wanted to be like. We both had such a laugh!

I always thought we would grow old together and be the "little old ladies up the street." I welcomed you into this world and thought I would be the one to welcome you to heaven. You told me one time that I reminded you of a little bird. I don't know why, but that has stuck in my mind all these years.

The hardest thing, Bootsie, is the "never again" part. I will never again hear your laugh or see that special mischief in your eyes that always reminded me of Dad. We will never again go to the mall or giggle and be silly. The world is such a beautiful, miraculous place. How could you leave all this?

I miss you, Bootsie. I really wish you were here.

You will always be my little Sunshine Girl.

Love,

Snooker

See You Tomorrow

When my family immigrated to Australia from Croatia, my younger brother was only four years old. What a sweet boy he was, excited about a new adventure, not a worry in the world. That's how I remember Enio, with smiles instead of sadness, carefree instead of confused.

Enio was all boy and everything that went with that. Getting scrapes and getting into scraps were the rules of the day. One afternoon when we were walking home from school, he decided to grab a ride on the back of a garbage truck. He jumped on and had the time of his life, until he fell off. He cut his knee so badly I could see all the way to the bone.

Often my mum would be cleaning his room and find moldy, uneaten sandwiches hidden in an old suitcase under his bed. We laughed about that for years to come. Enio never did take much time to eat. At school, lunchtime was playtime. Of course, school time was also playtime for him. Attention deficit/hyperactivity disorder (ADHD) was not heard of in those days, but his behavior was typical for those with ADHD.

No one knows if he was crying for help or if he really wanted to end his life, but I was too late when I ran to him in the darkness. He had hung himself. I screamed when I saw him. I tried to cut him down alone but needed help. I called for an ambulance. Then, out of nowhere, my brother's terrified three-year-old boy, Adrian, appeared from inside the house with his little arms outstretched.

In the midst of all my shock and terror, I had to somehow collect myself and pick him up to take him to the front garden, where I set him on the mailbox. He looked up and pointed to the moon and the stars, not realizing that he had just lost the most important person in his life. I pretended everything was okay. But nothing was; my brother hung only meters away in the backyard. The eight minutes it took for the ambulance to arrive seemed like a lifetime.

My friend also arrived, and took Adrian and me to my place. I had to get out the phone book and try to find one of our mum's friends to help me tell her the devastating news. There was no way in this world I could tell her myself. Three of my mum's friends ended up coming with me. I wanted to die as I stood outside and watched our poor mum open the front door, not knowing her heart was about to be broken. Mine already was.

That bundle of joy who came into my life in the Croatian village was now gone. I can still see my dear brother's face when he was a newborn, staring up at me from my mother's bed. That smile, that sweet smile. I will never forget it, and I know I will see it again one day.

Tiyana Mardesich
Enio's Sister

Enio Michael Lesinjani
Thirty-seven years old

Dear Brother,

I remember the day Mum brought you home from the hospital. I was three-and-a-half years old. I got the few toys I had and put them on the big double bed next to you so you could play with them. A baby brother! I thought we'd grow old together. I never imagined thirty-seven years later I'd help choose a coffin for you.

But it did happen. And now you are gone forever; gone from our lives, but not our hearts. I try to remember the good times, the times you made me laugh, the times you stirred my husband about his football team, the Bulldogs, and he stirred you back about your team, the Saints. Then you'd have a beer together and continue the footy debate. You were always happy when you came to our place. Family meant a lot to you, especially since little Adrian was born.

Mixing in with people was always hard for you, but after Adrian arrived, you made sure that you turned up at family gatherings. All my friends liked you. They thought you were a great guy. It's a pity you didn't believe that. You always thought so low of yourself.

I said the eulogy at your funeral. I did it for you. I wanted people to know how special you were, that you were a good man, that you weren't a loser who just did drugs and took the easy way out.

But I realized in the following weeks that not many people thought badly of you. Twenty of the guys from your work came to your funeral to pay their respects. They also collected six hundred dollars for your boys. They all thought of you as a good bloke. No one could believe what happened.

You had been extra happy that day at work. You phoned only two hours earlier that night to ask me if I could look after your new baby, Marcus, the next day while you and your partner did the weekly shopping.

I said, "Of course, no worries."

And you said, "See you tomorrow then."

I never imagined that those would be your last words to me. I miss you and love you.

Your sister

St. Patrick's Day Blessing

Halle was born with the luck of the Irish smiling down upon on her. But her Aunt Jennifer says it's not the Irish who are smiling. It's a proud father. A man Halle will never know. A man who hung himself in the basement of their home before she was born.

A happy child, popular in school and surrounded by a close, loving family, Josh grew into that same kind of man—a lover of life, someone who shared that love with all those around him. The consummate entertainer was quick to laugh and ready to help everyone else laugh right along with him.

Friends could count on jokes to be told over and over again on the softball field where Josh and his buddies spent most of their time after work, dreaming, perhaps, of a cheering crowd after hitting a homerun. After the game, the guys always went to "Pine Street," the bar that sponsored the team. A framed gray baseball jersey with the number five still hangs on the wall. That's Josh's jersey, signed by the entire team.

Jennifer always wanted to tag along with Josh, and like most brothers, he left her behind. He didn't think having his sister around was cool. But the pair still had a deep love for one another. They shared secrets, hopes, and dreams. To Jennifer's sadness, they never said enough about how much they cared for one another. They grew apart—by circumstance, not choice.

After Jennifer left for college, Josh changed. No longer a free spirit, he became angry and detached. Antidepressants helped for a while, but then he told his family that the medication made him feel as though he weren't the one in control. He felt like the pills took something from him, so he stopped taking them.

On some days, Josh seemed to have it all together, and on others it seemed nothing would ever be right again. His family was on an emotional roller coaster, not wanting to say the wrong thing to a man they used to be able to say anything to. Walking on eggshells was part of everyday life.

Josh was once a successful, career-oriented man, but then he suffered several layoffs. He was also in a new marriage, yet he still didn't know what he wanted out of life. Not even his close-knit family knew how desperate Josh was until the call he made to his pregnant wife, telling her of his plan. She found him in their basement seven minutes later, hanging from a rafter.

Since that hot July day, nothing has been the same for Jennifer or her family. She passes the ballpark where her brother used to play. She can still see him making jokes with players and pals. She wants to share those memories with Halle—the memories of how Josh lived like there were no tomorrows. Because after that July day, there were no tomorrows for Josh.

Jennifer holds on to the brother she loves so very much. She knows he is smiling down on her and Halle. They don't really need the luck of the Irish. Jennifer and Halle have Josh.

Joshua James Foust
Twenty-five years old

Dear Josh,

I just got home from seeing your daughter for the first time. I was very nervous about going over to your house. I haven't been there since you died. Halle looks exactly like you. She is the most beautiful little girl in the world. But she is going to have a rough life growing up without you.

You would have been a great dad, especially since you were a kid at heart. I always pictured you teaching your kids to ride a bike, taking them to Grandma and Grandpa's to go fishing, teaching them to play foosball, your favorite.

Even though I always complained about being known as "Josh's sister," I loved people knowing that. I was proud to stand next to you. When you left, you took a big part of us with you.

I am still not comfortable talking to Mom and Dad about how much I cry. It breaks my heart to see them in such pain. I never know what kind of mood they will be in. Grandma still sits and looks out the window, totally at a loss for words.

As I write this I don't even know what tense to use. I talk sometimes like you are still here. I find myself making mental notes about something I need to tell you, until, with a real slap in the face, reality sets in, and I realize I will never hear your voice again. When I hear a song on the radio that reminds me of you, I change the station.

Everyone says time will make things easier, but I'm finding it makes things harder. Each day I think about something I wish I would have said to you or a situation I want to erase. I think about the last time I saw you and how I acted toward you. I wasn't very nice. I was angry with you for not coming to my party and for not letting me borrow your coolers.

Some days I am extremely mad at you for being so selfish. Other days I can't even talk, afraid I'll start crying. I always get this weird feeling when I see people I know. I am afraid they will come up to me and ask how you are. How do I answer that?

"Well, I think he is at peace now. Didn't you hear? He killed himself."

Dad wanted to yell at you for doing what you did. Mom is trying hard to deal with all of this, but it is hard losing her only son and her father less than a year apart.

Josh, it is hard for your friends to do the things they used to do. I know they are having a hard time filling your shoes on the softball field. I know you are up there with "EZ," playing foosball and having a beer or two. It was a shame he took his own life the exact same way you did, less than two months after you. You both had so much to live for. But it is comforting knowing you are not alone.

Not a day will pass that you will not be thought of or missed. You were a special part of so many lives—lives that will never be the same. We will be a family again. We just have to be patient.

Your sister,

Jen

Hearts Made Us Friends

Pam was glowing that October evening. Earlier in the day she had taken a home pregnancy test and found out she was carrying her first child. She went to the store and bought a special bib with the words, "Baby is love." She put the bib on a teddy bear and gave it to her husband, Allen, when he got home that night. He was thrilled. They were going to bring a new life into this world!

Pam couldn't wait to share the joy with her younger sister and her parents. She announced the news by buying each of them a picture frame with the engraved words "A Baby to Love." She wrapped the frames and, without saying a word, handed each of them their gift. They understood right away. Her sister, Shirley, started crying, and the two hugged tightly.

Pam and Allen spent the next nine months preparing. They painted the nursery in beautiful pastels and set up the "Precious Moments" changing table, the light yellow crib, and the white lace bassinette. The room was ready to make their child feel safe and loved.

Pam had some morning sickness, but nothing out of the ordinary. However, by the end of her term, she had gained thirty pounds and was quite uncomfortable. She was a petite woman, and carrying around that extra weight put a strain on her back and heart. But it was all worth it when Melanie Amber arrived kicking and crying. She was perfect—blue eyes, brown hair, ten toes, ten fingers, and a set of strong lungs.

Pam was in tears as she held her new baby. She was crying because of the pain and because of the joy. Something she had dreamed about since she was a little girl was truly taking place. She was a mommy!

Within days, that contentment was replaced with confusion. Something was wrong. It seemed much deeper than the "baby blues," and Pam was deathly afraid. She told Shirley something just wasn't right. She knew she shouldn't be feeling that way. She should be warm and nurturing, not cold and uncaring.

Pam's family took her to the doctor. He prescribed the postpartum depression medication, Sarafem. He said if she took that and got some rest, she would be fine.

Shirley planned to go on a four-day vacation, but felt guilty for leaving her sister behind when she was so depressed. The doctor and her family encouraged her to go, assuring her Pam would be fine. Pam even told Shirley to go, since that was the only time she could take off from work.

Shirley will regret her decision forever, because she would never see her sister alive again. When she got home, she wanted to visit Pam, but Pam refused to let her stop by. Shirley learned from her family that Pam had become a shell of what used to be a vibrant and carefree woman. Depressed, hardly saying a word, she had a blank stare, and her sunken eyes gave her face a ghostly image.

Pam's medication was not helping. The next day Shirley called Pam's doctor and told him that her sister needed help immediately. Pam never made it to the doctor. She just couldn't hold on any longer. Exactly two weeks after giving birth to Melanie Amber, Pam put a gun to her head while her newborn screamed in her crib.

To this day, Pam's family doesn't talk about what happened. In fact, they don't even bring up the words suicide or postpartum depression. Instead, they smile around each other and cry alone behind closed doors.

Shirley's friends tell her that Pam had love in her heart. They say that love kept her from taking Melanie Amber's life as well. That does little to soothe Shirley, who feels lost without her big sister. But she is comforted to know that part of her sister will live on through Melanie Amber.

Talking about the last days of her sister's life is too difficult, but Shirley does talk about all the days before that. There is one gift she holds especially close. Pam gave her a heart-shaped plaque that reads: "Chance made us sisters, hearts made us friends." Shirley knows she is lucky to have had such a wonderful sister and friend, if only for a short time.

Pamela Huffman Smoak

Thirty-two years old

Pam,

I can't believe this has happened. I can't believe you are really gone. I find myself totally unable to accept this. You should be here with me. We should be having lunch together. We should be going places, doing things, all the sisterly things we used to do. Now all of that is gone. You are gone.

Realistically, I know that you are gone. I attended your funeral and approved the wording for the name plaque on your grave. I have visited your grave and have seen with my own eyes that your name is there.

I placed seashells on your grave from my most recent trip to the beach. Remember how we used to love the beach? I still think about the time we went to the beach together and jumped the waves. What a wonderful day! I have taken a flag with a beach scene on it to your gravesite. You loved the beach so much.

I also have that pretty angel statue out there that you ordered. It came in shortly after you were buried. I could have canceled the order beforehand, but I knew you wanted the statue, and I wanted you to have it.

Something evil has taken you away from me. My sister would have never intentionally caused anyone this much pain and suffering. I do not believe you were in your right mind at the time that you did this. You were suffering from postpartum depression, I know, but it would have gotten better, sweet Pam, if only you could have held on.

I am so sorry for the fight we had the year before this happened. I know we made up, but I am so sorry. We lost such precious time together, and I would give anything to be able to get that back. It doesn't matter now who was right or wrong. What truly matters is the time that we lost.

I am also sorry about leaving to go on vacation. I did not know you were suffering so much, or I would not have gone! I would never have left you there to suffer alone. I deserted you in your time of need. Everyone tells me not to blame myself, but I can't help thinking that I left you when you needed me the most.

I have dialed your phone number hoping you'd answer, but I was slapped in the face instead when a recording stated that your number had been changed. It listed your in-laws' number. I can't ride by your house. It hurts too much.

I don't know how to go on without my sister. I love you so very much. I hope you know that. I hope you can hear me. I hope you never doubted for one single minute how I felt and how I still feel about you. I love you with all of my heart and soul.

Forever & Always,

Shirley

Boardwalk in the Rain

Once you heard it, you could never forget it; his laugh was so spirited, so full of life, so contagious. People were attracted to Doug's all-American, boy-next-door good looks. But they were also drawn to his personality. He was forceful and commanding, yet sensitive and endearing. People flocked to him the way a child is drawn to a mother's arms.

Doug was a guy's guy, someone everybody liked. He was a regular Joe, who liked NASCAR's Jeff Gordon, wrestling's "Stone Cold" Steve Austin, and Aerosmith's Steven Tyler. But there was a softer, more unpredictable side to Doug that he shared only with his older sister Sophie.

They loved gardening and nature trails. Together they traveled the Maryland countryside, taking road trips and finding wooded areas and fields that called for them to come explore. But as they grew up, time took them in separate directions.

While Sophie was enjoying a new life with her husband, Doug was searching for his soul mate. The woman he thought was the one broke his heart one fall night. After a terrible fight, Doug stood in front of his parents' home and ended his life with a gun. He lay there in the yard, alone.

One of the last times Sophie heard her brother laugh was during a summer walk in the rain. The rain cooled them down as they talked on the boardwalk. The surf pounded the sand, while brother and sister created new memories.

That's the baby brother Sophie holds in her heart. That's her memory of Doug—the way he looked at her that day, the way he smiled, the way he laughed.

Doug E. Tompkins

Twenty-two years old

Sophie read this poem at Doug's funeral, while her father stood beside her.

We didn't get much time together,
The miles kept us apart.
But the phone calls and the times we did hang out
I will cherish in my heart.
I wanted to be mad at you,
But what good would that do?
I would rather think of you the way I did,
And that's always loving you.
Though no one person is to blame,
There's no explanation, no one knew your pain.
When I think of you, your trademarks and style,
I know it will always make me smile.
Our lives will never be the same.
I will stop and think whenever I hear your name.
Oh, the lives you have touched.
I know you're with people who loved you just so much.
It's our parents I feel sorry for,
Because no one, no one loved you more.
And now these miles we cannot part
But forever you will remain in my heart.

Sophie Metz
Doug's Sister

Bubba Shawn

Nick was the baby of the family. Shawn, Steven, Seth, and Sarah always made sure he knew it, too. They teased him and tossed him around, but they did it with love. They were the five musketeers.

Nick was so proud of his siblings. He found a special friend in each one. Steven taught him about computers. Seth shared his love of matchbox cars. Thanks to Sarah, Nick found respect for girls by taking part in Girl Scout outings with Sarah and her troop.

But it was Shawn he looked up to the most. Shawn was ten years older, and Nick believed he knew everything there was to know. However, there were two things in particular Shawn was passionate about: wrestling and video games. And he passed that passion on to Nick.

Together they would watch wrestling on television, cheering on their favorites and booing their enemies. Then the brothers would go head-to-head challenging each other to video games. Most of the time Shawn would win, but every once in awhile he would let his little brother take the victory.

Shawn never told him, but Nick was the apple of his eye. He never minded having his little brother around. He loved watching his bright eyes sparkle when he learned something new. Shawn even secretly loved Nick's name for him. The nickname actually started when Sarah was a toddler. She tried to say "brother," but it came out "Bubba." Sarah outgrew calling her brothers "Bubba," but Nick never did. He called the brothers, "the Bubbas." Shawn was forever "Bubba Shawn."

Nick was devastated when Shawn took his life that Saturday morning, but he found strength and guidance from Seth, Steven, and Sarah. Their encouragement gave him the ability to honor Shawn at his funeral. At just fourteen, he wrote a tribute to his brother. He was too emotional to read it at the service. Nick sat in that funeral home crowded with those who knew and loved Shawn, as his sister read the words Nick had written.

> You were always a good older brother—the best, in fact. Whenever I needed some good advice or just someone to hang with, you always made time for me and knew the right things to say. You taught me a lot about life in general and especially about video games. I recall the many hours we spent together at our old house when you lived with us, trying to beat each other in our favorite games. Later, at the apartment that you shared with Steve and Seth, we exchanged cheat codes and game moves over the phone, sometimes tying up our lines for hours, causing Mom and the other Bubbas to get quite upset with us. Neither of us cared; we enjoyed each other's company.

Sarah had to stop for a moment. She looked up and saw her little brother sitting there with his hands in his lap and his head hung low. Then she saw all the other faces in the room. Some she recognized; most she didn't.

She continued reading.

> Shawn encouraged me to be a success in school, to follow in his footsteps, to graduate and further my education. By his example of hard work and perseverance, he showed me that if I work hard enough for what I want, I'll get it. I only wish I had thanked him for his help more often. Most older brothers don't want to be bothered with their younger brother tagging along, but Shawn never seemed to mind my being with him. Shawn was a compassionate person with a kind and gentle heart.

Sarah stepped away from the podium. She folded Nick's note and handed it back to her little brother as she sat down beside him. Nick's eyes were filled with tears. When the service was over, he laid the words he had written in the coffin beside his brother. Then he said one final private good-bye to his "Bubba."

Shawn Daniel Cook
Twenty-four years old

> My Dearest Brother,
>
> I will miss you greatly. There will forever be a void deep within my heart. Although I will not see your smile or hear your laughter again in this lifetime, I will remember all that you and I have shared. I will eternally love you.
>
> Nick

Shawn's mother also wrote a letter to him. You can find that in "Parents Left Behind."

How Tight They Pinch

Peggy laughs every time she thinks about that Thanksgiving Day more than twenty years ago. It is one of the funniest memories she has of her sister, Pat. Peggy can smile about it now. Back then, everyone was too hungry to smile.

Pat got up early to prepare the turkey for their feast. Family was in from out of town, so before everyone woke up, she wanted to have a few things done. That included sending her husband to the bakery for donuts. Good thing, because one by one, the adults and kids wandered into the kitchen ready for breakfast.

This was the first time Pat had been able to play hostess for the family, and she wanted everything to be perfect. Her table was already set with a beautiful fall-inspired tablecloth and matching napkins in napkin rings. She even used her silver flatware and candelabras for the first time. She put burnt orange candles on the table, surrounded by a fresh flower arrangement. Pat wanted to make sure the family would always remember that Thanksgiving. She definitely succeeded.

As the ladies worked together in the kitchen chopping, slicing, and stirring, they laughed about how the guys were glued to the television watching football. They also talked about the children's activities and accomplishments, the latest gossip, and what they all wanted for the new year. Despite the organized chaos, they created a wonderful meal: dressing and gravy, macaroni and cheese, green beans, mashed potatoes, several salads, and Pat's mother's one-and-only banana pudding.

Everything was ready, so Pat called for her brother-in-law, Earl, to take the turkey out of the oven. The rest of the family went to wash up. They all met in the dining room, where Pat put homemade place cards on the table. The family laughed as they ran to find their names. Through all the giggles and shuffling of chairs, they heard: "It smells terrific!" "I'm starved." "Let's eat!" "Pat, the table is gorgeous."

All of a sudden, the only sound was the shriek coming from the kitchen. Earl had just placed what should have been a golden brown turkey on the serving platter. Instead, there sat a pasty, uncooked bird, limp from sitting in the cold oven for seven hours.

In all of her excitement, Pat had forgotten to turn on the oven. So instead of sitting down to turkey and dressing, the family had eggs and toast that Thanksgiving. Later that day, Pat got the chance to show off her cooking skills. She turned the oven on with the family looking over her shoulder. The turkey made a great late-night snack.

That day was a blessing in disguise, because they had only a few more Thanksgivings together. Five years later, Pat took her life. Marital problems and years of giving so much of herself to others and very little to herself came crashing in on her. Pat left a note to Peggy that read, "Until you've walked my path in my shoes, you cannot really know the terrain or how the shoes pinch."

Peggy will never know how tight Pat's shoes were, but she does know her sister is gone, and all she has are memories that bring laughter, smiles, and tears. When Peggy thinks of that crazy Thanksgiving Day, she has all three: laughter from the turkey that fought until the bitter end not to get eaten, smiles from the satisfaction of seeing her sister serve the fine meal they eventually ate, and tears from the sadness of missing the sister she loved so very much.

Patricia Ann Perkins Anderson

Forty-nine years old

Peggy wrote this letter shortly after Pat's death.

Pat,

I am so angry with you. I heard on television that writing you a letter might help me get over the anger. I don't think it is going to help, because I talk to you every day, telling you how mad I am.

I know you apologized to me, and everyone else, for being selfish in doing this. Yes, yes, yes, you were selfish. We would all like to do something just for ourselves at times, but you know, you have kids. Now Cindy and Scott are alone. They certainly don't have a father to turn to.

And that brings up another angry thought. Why in the hell did you allow that SOB to bring you to do this awful thing? He wasn't worth it. He stripped you of so much while you were married, and now he stripped you of being a mother.

Pat, Pat, Pat, I am so mad at you. And the nerve of you, talking to me just hours before you did this awful thing. You lied to me and your son. He blames himself because he felt something was wrong. He checked the sleeping pills and only found six. He said if you tried overdosing it couldn't hurt you that much. He never dreamed of the car situation.

You must have been planning this since your husband's birthday, when he told you there was no getting back together. I hope you didn't look down and see him at the memorial service. He acted so upset. What an SOB!

Yeah, I know how lucky I am to have my husband Earl. What a difference between the two men. You know what, Pat? Maybe you were right. I must be the stronger one. I don't allow Earl or anyone else to change me unless I feel good about it. And yet, you allowed your husband to change your mind about God and the church altogether, and about the other weird ways he thought and acted.

And Mother! What do you think she is going through? I know you apologized, but that is not enough. She was depending on you being around when she moved to Austin, and now you are gone.

People say time heals everything, but I don't know how I can heal from this. I've been told I could have done nothing to keep you from doing what you did. I wish I could believe that.

We had such a good time together when I was in Austin with you just weeks ago. I thought we could become even closer. Now that hope is all gone.

You asked me to take care of Cindy and Scott, and you know I will, but damn you. You should be here to take care of them.

Almost twenty years later, Peggy wrote another letter to Pat.

Dear Pat,

Well, it's been a long time since you chose to leave us. How do I feel toward you after all these years? Knowing the hurt you went through with your husband, I've tried to understand. After the shock and anger wore off, I tried to put myself in your shoes, but that didn't work.

The saying is, "Things happen for a reason. Something good will come out of this." Bull! I have not found a reason for your actions, and nothing good has come from your situation. Yes, I am still mad at you after eighteen years.

I see Cindy and Scott with their children and no grandmother. I feel guilty even to this day when I am enjoying my grandkids and know you are not. I've tried to stay close to Cindy and Scott, but buying gifts at Christmas and birthdays is not what I call close. Living two hundred miles away keeps us apart, and that hurts. I'm letting you and them down.

I shouldn't worry about letting you down. You sure as heck didn't worry about laying the burden on me to watch after your two kids. I don't mind looking after them, but I cannot replace you. I have prayed that you can't look down on earth and see what you are missing. You have grandkids. How you would have loved them.

I still cannot have your photo up in our home. It hurts so much to see you. I cannot listen to the song you played in the car that night either. If it comes on, I turn off the radio. I just picture you in that darn car with the photos of Cindy and Scott in your arms, listening to that song.

Pat, I wish I could speak with you just for a minute to ask how you could leave your kids. How did you make it to the car in the garage that night knowing you would never see them again? Your husband, I can understand, but not your kids. You loved and adored them as much as any mother on earth. Pat, how could you do this?

My eyes are full of tears, and I have had to throw a few things to get the anger and hurt out. Who am I angry with? I don't know. You, your husband, myself, and God, I think, for allowing this to happen. I cry about you just about as much today as I did eighteen years ago. A day does not go by without thoughts of you. Oh, how I wish this was a long nightmare and I could wake up and you would be back. As time goes by, I miss you even more.

I really could use a sister. I buy cards for you for different events and just throw them in a drawer. I used to write in them, address the cards to heaven, and drop them in the mailbox. But I was afraid someone might catch me and send me to the funny farm.

Pat, I am thankful for our wonderful time together. I love you, and I should have been more sensitive to your needs. I think I could have made a difference. I am still mad at myself for not being there for you, and I have to think about that for the rest of my life. I hope you have forgiven me.

Bye, Pat, and I wish you were here.

There Went My Hero

I was seventeen years old and drunk. I had been kicked out of my mom's, and my older brother, Robby, took me in. I was outside talking with a neighbor girl when the phone rang.

"It's for you," she said.

How did my sister find me, and why had she even bothered? When she got to my brother's I started asking questions, but the only response I got was, "Wait to talk to Mom."

Something was wrong. Strangely, suicide even crossed my mind. And so did Robby. A few weeks earlier, he and I had a conversation about a blanket that belonged to our cousin Markie. Robby had taken that blanket from Markie's room after he suicided. I felt privileged that Robby let me use it.

As I cuddled up, I thought about my cousin and the pain his death caused so many people, including my brother. I asked my brother if he had ever thought about taking his life. He assured me that he would never consider it. He said he would never put us through the same pain our cousin did.

When my sister and I got to our mother's home, I could feel the sorrow and pain that filled every crack and corner. A quiet fog covered my skin. My mother began telling me what happened. I stopped her mid-sentence to get permission to smoke.

She turned to her roommate for approval. He shrugged. He didn't know what to do. It all seems so surreal now. Who cared about cigarette smoke in the house when my brother was dead?

As I lit the wrong end of my cigarette, my mother stood up from the sofa and grabbed me. She pulled me close and whispered, "Your brother shot himself tonight."

I dropped to the ground, screaming, "I didn't mean it! I'm sorry! I didn't mean it!"

A few days earlier, Robby and I had a fight. I was so mad that I tore his apartment apart, figuring that would teach him. But he was actually trying to teach me. He knew I did drugs, and he didn't approve. I was living under his roof, and he said if I didn't stop using, he was going to throw me out. I said things I now wish I could take back.

"I hate you! I wish you weren't my brother! I wish you were dead!"

As I stood there in my mother's arms, I smelled the cigarette smoke drifting up to my nose and felt the wetness of the tears dropping from my eyes. The tears then stopped just as suddenly as they had started. I went upstairs to bed and stared at the ceiling. I couldn't sleep. All I could do was think about the last time my brother and I talked.

I couldn't cry again. It wasn't that I didn't love my brother or didn't care. Part of me was saying, "He's dead. No more fighting. He can't hurt me anymore." At the same time, his death would hurt me forever. There was no making up this time.

The next day I saw the spot where he shot himself. Still, nothing would come, not even one tear. We flew to Michigan for the funeral, where my sister and I were in charge of the music. We picked out some of his favorite songs as well as some songs that we felt were appropriate for the "occasion." Even through all of that, I didn't cry.

At the funeral I sat in my reserved seat waiting for the service to start. The Mariah Carey song "Hero" started playing, and that's when I broke down. Finally. I sobbed uncontrollably. I just couldn't hold it in. My whole body hurt.

After the funeral, everyone had a chance to say good-bye. I was the last one left. I held my brother's hand as I laid a poem I had written for him at his side. I looked down at Robby and whispered in his ear, "Please wake up. Robby, wake up."

All I remember after that is three people pulling me away, telling me it was time to go. I blacked out. I was told I was hitting and punching him. I hear it gets easier with time, but not for me. It gets harder every day.

One day something good will come from this, but not right now. Right now, I still feel seventeen. I am drunk and mad at my brother. But he is my one and only hero—a hero I lost that cold November day. Maybe he knows that now.

Christa Slade
Robby's Sister

Robby James Wirick
Twenty-seven years old

Dear Robby,

It's been more than three years since you left us. I can't say the pain has gone away or even that it's gotten better. I can't even say I'm not still angry with you. Some days I am more angry with you than when you first died.

I'm turning into a woman, and you're not here to see it. I have two kids, a boy who is two and a girl who is seven months. My son looks a lot like you did as a baby. My daughter is such a beautiful princess. You would be so proud of them.

I don't have my big brother anymore. I can't just pick up the phone to call you for advice. Our kids can't play together. You took a piece of my life with you. I still cry for you. Sometimes when I'm driving I think I see you in the lane next to me. Or when I'm in a crowd I think I hear you laughing behind me.

As time passes, I remember less and less of you. I promised myself that I would never forget, but it's hard. My heart hurts. No one fully understands why.

I am twenty-one, and I will never heal from this pain. Some days it feels as though it will never get easier. You're supposed to be here today. We're supposed to get together to talk about life and our problems, and then laugh about it all. We're supposed to get into fights, but you're not here. I scream at the walls, wishing those walls were you.

I tried my whole life to make you proud, and now you are not even here to see me grow up! It's hard to think that I will be older than my big brother. It's not supposed to be like that. You broke a promise to me. You promised you would never do this to me. I still don't understand why you left us. You are so damn selfish! All you could think about was yourself, your pain. You could not even think of us, your babies, or the family and friends who loved you more than anything.

Oh, how I would do anything to hug you or to hear your voice one more time. I miss you more than words could ever express. I feel so empty. When I think of you, there is a void, a void that I can never fill, no matter how hard I try.

If I could have had a few minutes to say a few last words to you, I would have told you that I'm sorry. I would have told you how important you were to me and how lucky I felt to be able to say, "Hey, that's my big brother." You are special to me, and that will never change. I love you! Those three words sum it all up. I love you!

Christa

Robby's mother also wrote about the loss of her son. You can read her story in "Parents Left Behind."

Mona Lisa in a Silver Frame

It was a beautiful summer afternoon in Amsterdam. The family gathered in a park for a wedding anniversary. The nine grown children were honoring their parents' three decades of commitment, hoping their own relationships could last as long and be as happy.

The greatest gift the family got from that gathering was not one wrapped in pretty paper with a big bow on top. It was one that came weeks later. Lya was putting together a photo album for her parents so they could remember that special day. She had dozens of candid shots of family and friends.

In one particular photo, Lya noticed an unusually special shot of her already beautiful younger sister, Yvonne. The golden-haired girl needed little to help her beauty, but at the moment that picture was taken, the sun perfectly lit the back of her hair, giving Yvonne an angelic glow. It was the most beautiful photo Lya had ever seen.

Her sister's smile was one of quiet serenity and inner peace. Her skin was radiant, her eyes clear blue pools that carried anyone who dared stare into them deep into her soul. The photo reflected incredible security, as well as infinite sadness.

Several years later, Lya moved with her husband and children to China. She was unpacking a bedroom filled with cardboard boxes. Sitting on her bed, she looked over at a boxed labeled, "Lya - Personal." She knew what was inside, so she took a deep breath and slowly got off the bed.

She carefully cut the tape, then lifted the box's four flaps and reached inside. Surrounded by bubble wrap, packing tissue, and a velvet cloth, was a framed photo.

With the frame still wrapped in velvet, Lya carried it over to the bed. She gently unwrapped it. The face of her lovely sister, Yvonne, stared back at her. The beautiful one. The smart one. Lya cleaned the glass with the velvet cloth and set the photo on the bedside table.

Lya then heard voices coming down the hall toward her, so she quickly tried to compose herself. She did not want her family to know she was upset. More than twenty years had passed since Yvonne died, but the anniversary of her death was still very hard. Even with so many years gone by, this day was particularly hard.

Straightening herself, Lya stood up and put on a smile. She looked down at the photo, kissed her fingers, and then touched her sister's face. The voices in the hall were now right outside her door. Then a knock.

"May we come in, Mom?"

Wiping away a tear, Lya moved toward the door. "Of course."

The door burst open. "Happy birthday to you. Happy birthday to you. Happy birthday, Dear Mom. Happy birthday to you."

Lya began to cry again, only this time out of love, not sadness. It was her birthday. It was also the day her sister suicided. Birthdays are hard for her, but Lya wants them to be happy memories for her family.

Her children led her toward the kitchen for her birthday cake. As she walked out of the bedroom, Lya glanced over her shoulder at her sister's smiling face.

"Until I see you again, little sister. Happy Birthday to me."

Yvonne Van Lieshout
Twenty-one years old

Dear Sweety,

It's my birthday, but, of course, you know that. Time to celebrate? I don't think so, and you know why. It's just not nice to celebrate birthdays anymore. You left us on my birthday so many years ago, and I never got over it. Why did you choose that day?

I've now reached an age that sometimes makes me a bit scared to look in the mirror. I dislike promises that are never going to be kept, like those television commercials showing how easy it is to get rid of wrinkles and stuff. Silly me, I bought miracle creams, oils, and masks, but I have to admit, there's nothing that will hide my age, no matter what. It's a waste of money, a waste of time, and a waste of energy.

You kept your decision so well hidden. A million times I said to myself, if only I had known, but I didn't. It might have been a bit easier for you, as well as for me, if you had shared your life with me. What made you choose to leave us? Who harmed you so much? What made you so unhappy?

It must have been a hell of a job to wear the mask just to convince us you were happy. Everyone feels once in awhile that life is hard. We all have wishes that something will change, but nothing changes if we don't work on the things that cause us misery and loneliness. I hope you gave yourself a chance to work out the things that made you feel like a failure. You were never a failure. Never.

At this point in my life, I can look at your photo without being mad at you for leaving us. But thousands of days have gone by with not only my sadness, but also my anger toward you, because I longed for you, and you left. Didn't you know that your decision was a very permanent one for a very temporary problem?

I want yesterday back, and I want you back. I have that same thought every night before I close my eyes. Then I say good-bye to you, followed by my simple words: "If only . . ."

I will love you forever, Princess, with your Mona Lisa smile.

Please keep watching over me,

Lya

Help to Heal a Sibling's Heart

These letters, poems, and stories overwhelm me. Heartfelt emotion, so true, raw, and powerful, humbles me as a professional psychologist. My observations are from a secular and psychological point of view. Notwithstanding such possibilities as an immortal soul, an afterlife in heaven, or even the resurrection of the departed, I have a personal version of surviving suicide. It is to cope with the traumatic event in ways that, while they may change over time, are least harmful to all survivors, and involve family and friends.

The narratives and stories of suicide in this section reveal a prolonged, relentless kind of grieving. It goes on apace, waxing and waning continuously for months and years, even decades. Reminders of loss, such as photos, videos, children, and parents, are woven inextricably into both joyous and sad memories.

It is so easy and natural to take suicide personally: "He got even with me." "She tried to hurt *me* and left *me* a legacy of lifetime hurt." Perhaps true, but such feelings detract us from the frustration and misery that may have prompted the act in the first place.

Initially, shock, disbelief, and fear may dominate; then anger pops up, again and again. A role model is gone, and the fun is drained from family occasions like Thanksgiving, Christmas, or birthdays (see "Mona Lisa in a Silver Frame"); the pain is compounded by never seeing or talking to the deceased again.

The intimate letters collected here underscore the central point that brothers and sister are active, complicated, and important figures in each

145

other's lives—not just on holidays, but every day. From childhood, they cooperate, fight, teach, admire, and often secretly love each other much more than they are willing to admit. Sudden death prompts the survivors to acknowledge the depth of feelings usually hidden in the rush of daily life (see "Dial M for Mistake").

Inside families, brothers and sisters may try to outshine each other, so the underlying tenderness and respect remains unsaid or ignored. The letters in this section capture the positive feelings, the admiration, and the reflected love that emerge in a shared environment (see "Red, White, and Bootsie").

The poignant and immediate impact for family members of suiciders may involve psychological trauma for brothers and sisters. Startling disturbances in feelings, behaviors, or dreams contrast with family and friends who avoid or minimize the event. Even if terminal illness (see "Here's to You, Jude") or senility is involved, the trauma can be horrific. So, in addition to the often mentioned psychiatrist or psychotropic medication, professional counseling for the family and close friends should be considered. Recall EZ who suicided two months after Josh (see "St. Patrick's Day Blessing").

Our attention in these stories and letters is drawn to the time perspective: past, present, and future. Tears come to our eyes when we hear siblings reflect on an impossible future—children graduating and marrying, sharing family events, growing old together. Natural as it is to look ahead, what *was*, in this case, is so much more gratifying and realistic. We recall the strong voices, vibrant mood, and important roles of the deceased, as well as the joy, warm memories, jokes, and even the arguments.

The sudden, unexpected suicide of a brother or sister permanently shuts down direct communication. Guilt and shame are so potent, not only due to the stigma of suicide, but to a sibling's sense of obligation. Most of us know in our minds that we are not responsible for another person's life, but in our hearts the feeling persists that somehow, someway, we could have helped. We wonder how we could have been betrayed by a brother or sister hiding such a profound act.

Writing letters opens us up to our deepest feelings and most important recollections. We can pick up the relationship as it was, share our reactions, raise questions, apologize, say farewell, and keep some part of the friendship alive. In many cases, the positive, loving memories persist and predominate over a long period of time. An ongoing diary or journal encourages survivors to observe and evaluate changes in recall, anger, and resentment. Over time, those emotions may be replaced with love, respect, and longing for the other person (see "There Went My Hero").

It's hardly inspirational, but I want to leave you with some notions that I've termed **PARD**—steps that form a scaffold to fill out in your own way.

Protect yourself from undue anxiety, guilt, and depression following a suicide, and especially from the wish to join your dead brother or sister. If counseling, medication, self-help groups, or other forms of assistance are needed, don't hesitate to avail yourself of them.

Accept the fact that you will, in all likelihood, never know all you want to know about a suicide. Misunderstanding, ambiguity, confusion, and simply inadequate information are commonplace.

Reject any idea that you caused the suicide or that you should, or could, have prevented it. Even with the best treatment for depression, suicide occurs.

Detect and evaluate any undue pressure in yourself to restore the tarnished image of a brother or sister who suicides. Realistic appreciation is appropriate in the long run, but question yourself if you want to go to extremes. We all possess attractive and unattractive characteristics, alive or dead.

I leave you with these thoughts and my encouragement.

Dr. Norman S. Giddan, PhD[1]

---

1. Dr. Norman S. Giddan, clinical psychologist and psychotherapist, has served as the director of mental health at Florida State University and the University of Toledo. In private practice now for over ten years, Dr. Giddan has edited and written half a dozen nonfiction books on psychological development and treatment.

Shadow from a Sunset
Friends Left Behind

"Blood Brothers"

Often I think back
    To when we were young
Always together
    Searching for fun
Tested through time
    Bonded for life
We became brothers
    Cut from a knife
With hands gripped tight
    He looked in my eye
Brothers we are
    Now 'til we die

—Wade Hendricks
    Songwriter

The War and the Wall

Decades after the fighting ended, another casualty fell from the Vietnam War. This one didn't occur halfway around the world. This death was in Texas. Michael H. McBurnette was a US Air Force veteran who served with the 602nd Air Commando Squadron in the Republic of South Vietnam. He had just begun to explore his experiences in Vietnam when he took his life during early morning hours in a remote area outside of Houston.

Michael was a kind soul and my friend. He was affiliated with the Vietnam Veterans of America's Houston Chapter 343, where he helped organize the first Veterans' Day event ever held in the Texas Department of Criminal Justice (TDCJ). He accomplished that just two months before he took his own life.

Perhaps he felt compassion for his fellow service members behind bars because he knew what being incarcerated was like. Michael was imprisoned by a war he could not forget but did not want to remember. Michael sometimes spoke with me about life after Vietnam. He talked of sleepless nights and daytime demons. As many people do, Michael tried self-medicating with alcohol, but soon discovered that that path held many more demons.

It was not easy, but Michael eventually mastered his own recovery and became a substance abuse counselor with the TDCJ. However, while helping others, he rarely spoke of his own personal battles, not even with the Rescue and Recovery Group with whom he served. His talks with me became fewer and fewer.

If Michael had brought his fears and feelings out into the open, he would have had to deal with them. He wasn't ready to do that. Still,

Michael was able to help others find their way to sobriety. He knew what an inmate was feeling, because he could speak of his own difficulty with alcohol and addiction. He was an inspiration to many because he truly cared for his fellow man.

But on that January morning, Michael was in need. He could no longer fight the demons, and he could not face another day. Alone, Michael ended his life.

I am angry with Michael right now. He took my good friend away before I was ready to let him go. I am angry he did not let us know of his pain. I am even angrier that we did not see his pain. Someday, I will be able to forgive Michael for leaving, but not yet.

Even though he is gone, Michael continues to help others. Donations in his name were made to Chapter 343's Veterans' Assistance Fund. His clothing was distributed to homeless veterans.

But perhaps his most enduring legacy was the decision made by the inmates in TDCJ's Jester III unit. The first Vietnam Veterans of America Incarcerated Veterans Chapter in the TDCJ system is known as the Michael H. McBurnette Memorial Chapter. Michael would like that.

Michael was cremated, and his ashes were left at The Wall in Washington DC. This is only fitting and proper. As so many other veterans before him who could not "survive the surviving," he, too, deserves to be immortalized with the 58,000 names inscribed there for generations to see and remember.

Michael may not have his name on The Wall, but his name is inscribed in the hearts of those who knew him. Michael was very proud that he was a Vietnam veteran. I am very proud he was my friend.

Lynda Greene-Kahler
Michael's Friend

Michael H. McBurnette
Forty-eight years old

These words were written about Michael in a joint effort by inmates he counseled and befriended. They called him Mac.

"Stuff for Mac"

My friend Mac was a big man. You knew when he was in the room.
His smile was huge and warm. He would gladly give it to you.
The bravery was clear to see. He spent his tour in the DMZ.
He never doubted any man in white.
With a little help, we could see the light,
But he had to go, and he couldn't say good-bye.
He left us here to wonder why.
What tragedy couldn't he face?
What pain drove him from the human race?
Life is hard and wounds us all.
My friend Mac turned his pain toward helping others,
Until he couldn't take it anymore.
I think his heart was way too big.

Incarcerated Veterans
Ramsey One Unit, Rosharon, TX

Friends Never Leave

It was Christmas break, and we had been partying for a week straight. There was only one day left of our break, and we decided to have one more blowout. If I had known what would happen that night, I wouldn't have gone out. I saw something no one should ever see, especially at the age of sixteen.

I was supposed to be home at midnight, but I missed curfew. Around four in the morning, my friend Lee went home. He lived four doors down from where we all were. Another friend said I should go home, too, and offered to walk me. But I didn't want to go. I thought I might miss something. What happened later was something I wouldn't have minded missing.

The same friend who had been trying to get me to leave came into the living room screaming at the top of his lungs. No one could really understand what he was saying. All we could make out was Lee's name.

The guys told the girls to wait there while they went to see what was wrong. But we didn't wait. One by one we ran into the basement of the apartment building. When we got there, we saw some people standing in disbelief, some screaming, some crying.

I almost threw up. One of my friends grabbed my arm, and we took off, banging on doors until someone let us in to call 911. By the time we got back, Lee's body had been carried upstairs and was on the living room floor. About twenty of us sat around him and cried. We hugged each other and prayed he would be all right. Before he was put in the ambulance, I put my hand on Lee's chest and said, "Don't go."

I honestly don't remember walking home that morning. I was in such a daze, like the whole thing was a horrible dream and any minute I was going to wake up. I tried to sleep but couldn't. I just stayed in bed and called a few of my friends who hadn't already heard what had happened.

Two days later the visitations started. It was so hard to understand what was going on, because every single one of my friends was grieving. We were all in the same kind of bad shape, so talking to them didn't do me much good.

As a final goodbye, we all wrote something on a piece of paper and put it in Lee's casket. Then we all stood in front of those at the service and said The Lord's Prayer.

Lee was at rest. Everything was finally over. What I didn't know was that it was just the beginning for me. I couldn't go to sleep at night without seeing Lee's face. Every time I drove down that street, I couldn't even breathe. I saw the cops and ambulances and my friends on their knees praying to God. Then I went through a long period of shock and depression.

Now, a year later, after losing three more people—one on the first anniversary of Lee's death—I can finally sit down and talk about this. I am trying to find some good in it. I know we have a guardian angel looking over us all.

Everyone left behind after losing someone to suicide is a survivor. They are the ones left to pick up the pieces. Stay strong, and remember these four things.

Number one: the days that seem unbearable will get better, and you will get through them.

Number two: no matter how hard you think your life is or how bad you think you have it, someone out there always has it worse.

Number three: remember that whatever you are going through,

someone else is going through the same thing somewhere. You just have to find that person.

Number four: don't ever think your problems are so bad that you have to end your own life, because you're not only hurting yourself, you're hurting everyone who loves you. You may not think they love you, but they really do. Don't kill yourself to find out how much.

Kaylen Denning
Lee's friend

Lee Joa
Twenty years old

This is the note Kaylen left in Lee's coffin.

> Lee, well, where do I start? I am not going to really put anything sad on this, cuz I know that's not what you wanna hear. We had some awesome times together, and I am going to miss you with all my heart. I am glad I got to spend the last night you were here with you. I love you!
>
> Love, Kaylen

"Sealed with a Tear"

Marked with sadness and sealed with a tear,
 In my mind, crying and screaming is all I can hear.
We hugged and whispered it would all be okay,
 When we knew it wouldn't and still isn't to this day.
I can still see you lying there breathless on the floor.
 I can still hear the police banging on the door.
I can still feel the soft hands wiping my tears away.
 I can still smell our fear from that very day.
As we watched you lie there, we knew you were gone.
 Why did God do this to us? What did we do wrong?
Not a day has passed, not a single minute gone by,
 When I haven't asked myself why you wanted to die.
I know you are happy and in a better place.
 I swear at your funeral you still had a smile on your face.
I watched your baby pick up a picture of you
 And hold it in her hand.
What do we tell her? How will she ever understand?
 I will tell her about you, what an awesome guy you were.
And I'll make sure she knows this had nothing to do with her.
 So until I see you again, Lee, promise me you'll take care.
I am starting to accept this, but I know it's not fair.
 Keep partying, Lee, I know you know what I mean,
Until next time, I will see you in my dreams.

Kaylen Denning

Soul Sisters

Midday phone calls about everything and nothing. Laughter. Gossip. Kitchen-table conversations. Midnight ice cream runs. Husbands. Affairs. Early-morning workouts. Girls' night out. Love. Children. House-work. Responsibility. Heartbreak.

Female friendships are like no others. The women who find their soul sisters are the lucky ones. That almost didn't happen for Tonya and Pam. Both very young, they had just become part of the working world. Tonya was scared and insecure, Pam pretty and poised. Tonya saw Pam's confidence as conceit. Pam's great looks and quiet nature gave Tonya and her friends plenty to gossip and giggle about.

Pam held her head high and acted as if she didn't care that no one talked to her and that everyone talked about her. But inside, she desperately wanted a friend. Tonya saw the hurt Pam tried to bury, and she felt guilty. It was her fault Pam had no friends. So one day during a lunch break, Tonya swallowed hard, took a chance, and asked Pam to sit with her.

That was all it took to break down the wall between the two. They became inseparable. Tonya learned Pam was nothing like she had pictured. She was not a rich, spoiled little girl. In fact, she left home at the age of sixteen and ended up a bride abused by her husband. That was a far cry from what Tonya had imagined.

Instead of being worlds apart, the women were mirror images of each other. Both struggled to pay the bills, stayed with cheating husbands, and worked jobs that went nowhere fast.

Their friendship grew strong; there was no judgment, just unconditional love. The two were part of each other's lives for more than twenty years.

But one night, heartache overpowered Pam. Another cheating spouse, another drink, another unpaid bill. She could not handle another blow. Her spirit had been stolen by life's hard knocks.

Pam let death win late one February night.

She was staying with her brother, and they had company over. That's when Pam politely excused herself and went to bed early. She walked upstairs alone to her room, wrote Tonya a note, and put a pillow over her face. Pam's brother found her with a gun lying beside her.

Now it's Tonya who is crying for a friend. She thinks about Pam, smiles for what they had, and then cries for what they will never have. No more phone calls. No more late nights. No more midnight ice cream runs. But there are also no more cheating husbands. There is no more anger. No more punishment. When Pam died, Tonya gained her strength, and now she fights for a better life for both of them. Friends forever.

Pamela Renae Kistler
Thirty-nine years old

Pam,

As I sit here staring at this blank page, so many things go through my mind. Should I write about when we met? Should I write about all the fun times and struggles we had? Or should I write about how I feel since you left this world by your own hand? I think I'll do them all. I have plenty of time.

The last time I spoke to you was the day Dale Earnhardt died. Little did I know, you would soon join him in heaven. He was your hero. You called me crying so hard. We talked on the phone for over two hours. You finally calmed down. You said you felt the best you had in a long time. Had you made up your mind to end your life?

We had a great conversation—one I'll never forget. We cried, we laughed; I truly believed you were going to be okay. God, how stupid I was. I remember I was just getting off my morning break at work when the phone rang. It was your mom. I stood in the break room and listened; I remember thinking it couldn't be true.

Did you go to sleep and then wake up and do this? Did you go to your room with full intention of doing this? What threw you over the edge that night? Did you and your brother argue? No one who was there will talk about it. Maybe one day they will.

I miss you so much. So many unanswered questions haunt me every day. Did I do all I could? Did you do this to get even with the ones who hurt you all these years?

I know in my heart you didn't do this to hurt me. But, buddy, you sure have. I'm left to deal with all the jerks who ever hurt you in your life. Believe me when I tell you it's hard. I know you understand. I love you with every inch of my heart and soul. They can take all the material things away, but no one will ever take the memories we made. Our memories are what keep me going.

Till I see you again, I love you and miss you terribly. How about sending me back that piece of my heart you took with you?

Forever in my heart and soul,

Your bestest buddy,

Tonya

Weaving Words

Patchwork pieces create a colorful tapestry, complicated when looked at closely, but continuous when examined from afar.

Each person's life has that same piecework, reflecting the shapes and sizes of those who come into our lives. Some pieces fit; some don't. Regardless, all the pieces become a permanent part of our patchwork.

How each piece adds to or takes away from the overall creation is often not seen until the last stitch has been made. Mary Van Wychen and Gary Bloy are part of each other's tapestries. They were woven together through no choice of their own when Mary's sister became Gary's emotional punching bag.

Gary can easily be seen in Mary's tapestry. His piece is black and heavy and leaves her cold and angry.

Gary Alan Bloy
Thirty-seven years old

> Gary,
>
> It sounds horrible, but I'm glad you're dead. You would have made Susan's life hell. You knew they wanted a psychological exam and had it scheduled for Monday. You killed yourself on Saturday. You were a total coward! You were selfish, sick. I saw what you were doing to Susan and the kids. How dare you shove your sick thoughts on your kids. They loved you!
>
> Your thoughts were for yourself. You hurt our family. You tried to kill us. You hurt your kids. They don't want to be compared to you. You left them fatherless. Your death was both a blessing and a pain. Even in death you continue to

haunt all of us. Hopefully Susan will feel good enough about herself to get her life together.

You know what, though? You didn't scare me. Susan and the kids will move on. You will be a memory for your kids. You have lost out on the life you could have had with them. You got what you deserved, Gary. You brought it all down on yourself.

We won't speak ill of you with the kids. They will decide for themselves as they get older. I will love them and care about them. I will be here for them and do all the things you didn't want us to do. Too bad, Gary; yours was the wrong choice.

Your "crabby" sister-in-law,

Mary

Mary's sister, niece, and nephews also wrote letters to Gary. You can find them in "Loves Left Behind" and "Children Left Behind."

The Music Never Ends

Their friendship began in a middle school music room—one with cream-colored walls, black metal chairs, and dented music stands. A storage closet pushed into a corner locked away dreams, desires, and destinies. It was where drums, horns, and strings sat on wobbly wooden shelves.

Tony never went to the storage closet for his instrument. He kept his well-guarded saxophone in a black shiny case. It was the prize he purchased with money saved from birthdays, holidays, and countless lawns mowed every weekend since he was eleven.

Maria-Felix didn't have the money to buy her own bass guitar, so she used a well-worn one shared by other students. It was in her hands most of the time, just as it was the day she met Tony. He was tall, talented, and very handsome. She knew then that they would make the perfect pair in the jazz band.

Maria-Felix had already heard Tony perform. She had seen him control a crowd with his saxophone. He could take them to another place and time; make them smile, make them cry. Johnny Coltrane, Charlie Parker, Ben Webster—his name would surely follow theirs.

The bond between Tony and Maria-Felix grew strong quickly. Teachers were used to the two slipping off to the music room to jam during lunch period. Getting them to put up their instruments was a chore. Getting them to practice wasn't. Their three R's were reading music, writing songs, and keeping rhythm.

Middle school flew by for the friends; high school brought them closer. They became part of a bigger jazz band, performed in even more shows, and watched standing room only concert crowds move to their beat. Then came the performance all students looked forward to—playing at the graduation ceremony.

Tony was supposed to walk across the stage while his bandmates played on. He was supposed to go to college with a music scholarship. He was supposed to do a lot of things, but those things never happened. He never made it that far.

Maria-Felix will never forget the first time she had to walk into her high school music room alone—a room very much like the one where she and Tony met. The same metal chairs. The same beat-up instruments. She doesn't understand why Tony took his life. But she does know he is happy now—happy because he has joined those famous saxophonists for a jam session in heaven.

The only sound Maria-Felix hears from Tony now is the rustling of his red and black graduation tassel that hangs above his grave—the tassle he should have worn. This is where Maria-Felix comes to write music, right beside the friend she played with for so long.

John "Tony" Anthony
Seventeen years old

My Forever Dearest Tony,

I went to visit you on the one-year anniversary of your death. I want to tell you everyone still loves you and misses you deeply. There hasn't been a day when I haven't thought of you.

A couple of weeks ago, we went to Columbia for jazz band. I remember when we went in middle school. That was so fun. You climbed down the Moaning Taverns, and I couldn't go because I didn't have my parents there. I'm so glad we got stuck carpooling together for a lot of the trips. I had a lot of good times with you. I hope I can still remember them when I get old.

Next week we're going to Southern California to compete. I still have all of those pictures from when we went before. I'm really glad I got to know you, Tony. You're a really great guy.

I always looked up to you because you were the most honest person to be around. You're the only guy I didn't have a problem talking to. In fact, I don't think we ever argued or got mad at each other. We were great friends, Tony.

As I sit here writing this letter, I'm thinking back to all of our memories. The one that sticks out the most is your fifteenth birthday party. Everyone wanted me to go swimming, but I didn't have anything to wear, so they just threw me in!

I want you to know that I will always love you and miss you. Thank you for being the best friend that you were. I couldn't ask you for anything more.

When my time comes, I want you to be waiting for me with your saxophone, because I'm going to have my bass, and we're gonna jam for the rest of our afterlives.

Watch over all of us who are waiting to see you once again. You're always in my heart and on my mind. Take care. I love you.

Always and forever your friend,

Maria-Felix

Forever Missed

Have you ever had a friend who completely understood and accepted you? Someone who laughed even when your jokes were anything but funny? Someone who held your hand, or your hair, when you were sick? Someone who stood up for you in front of others even when she knew you were wrong? That was the friendship between Cherie and me.

We met in Banff, Alberta, through friends. And friends—boy, did Cherie have a lot of them. She knew most of the people in Banff and is the reason I know so many people. Cherie had one of those personalities everyone is attracted to. She always knew how to put people at ease.

If we were out with friends and she saw someone who was uncomfortable, she would spend the rest of the night making sure that person had a good time. And by the time Cherie was finished, that lonely person always did.

I wanted to be just like her. I admired Cherie's loyalty and honesty. I had never known anyone so committed to her friends. She would have done anything for someone in need. In fact, she seemed to care more about her friends than she did about herself. I will never be able to figure that out.

Cherie will always be the greatest thing that ever happened to me. I feel blessed to have known her. If I could go back and have the choice of meeting her and losing her all over again, or not meeting her at all, with all my heart I would do it over again. Our friendship was worth the pain.

Cherie was a blessing, and she taught me more than she will ever know. She taught me to not be scared of love, and how to show my feelings. She taught me to be who I am and not to be ashamed or embarrassed.

She also taught me something she will never know: she taught me that I wanted to be just like her.

I was meant to meet Cherie, and I am so thankful she was in my life, even if it was for just a few short years. So I choose not to reflect on the negative things that happened or those things that led to her death. I choose to reflect on the unforgettable happy times we had together. Those memories will never die. They will live in my heart, with Cherie, forever.

Kristin Lee Ross
Cherie's Friend

Cherie Lynn Farrell
Twenty-four years old

Life is full of many miracles,
    And you came to us as one.
Left your handprints on our hearts,
    Filled our spirits with your sun.
Too good to get the hard life,
    But you battled it and won.
Embraced the world with your beautiful creation,
    And left us when you were done.
Seduced us with charm, flattered us with bliss,
    Everyone you touched got a taste of heaven's kiss.
Sent to earth for a reason,
    Our mentor, our friend,
Forever missed.

Kristin Lee Ross

Little Boy Lost

At the age of seventeen, he became a father to an angelic baby girl named Callie. She was so much like her father, with beautiful blue eyes and a heartwarming smile. Jason Dean Andresen said she was the best thing he had ever done. He was just a kid himself when he took his life with a shotgun. He just couldn't imagine that the pain and heartache would ever end.

That Jason seems so different from the one who had existed just a few years before. A good student who made mostly A's, he was devoted to baseball, wrestling, football, and basketball. By the time he reached high school, he was taking college courses as part of a talented teen program. Jason was very competitive and always wanted to be the best.

But at fourteen, something happened. Life was no longer the storybook "happily ever after" with Mom and Dad, family vacations, and weekend barbeques. His parents divorced. His father moved out, and his mother was bitter and drank too much. She then started verbally abusing Jason.

Jason felt like he couldn't do enough to please his mother. She kicked him out of the house several times, forcing him to find shelter in the freezing night air. Once, he even slept in the yard under a picnic table. Jason cried a lot and tried to run away, but he kept coming back, thinking things would get better.

Jason was a quarterback on the high school football team, and he was trying to get a scholarship. He thought that would be his ticket out, but he couldn't have been more wrong. He was sacked during a game, and a doctor told him his shoulder would never be the same; he would never be able to throw as hard or as far, and his aim would never be as true.

Eventually Jason dropped out of high school, giving in to his overwhelming depression. Unemployed and drifting, he had only one bright spot. He was in love with a beautiful girl. And when they became pregnant, they took responsibility. He was overwhelmed, but he was also overjoyed.

Their daughter, Callie, was born almost three months prematurely. She was in the hospital for quite some time. Jason made the hour-and-a-half drive to and from the hospital almost every day. He watched videos that taught him how to take care of his tiny daughter. Jason loved her with all his heart.

Because Jason had no steady income, his girlfriend's mother talked him into letting her adopt Callie. She told him her insurance would pay the medical bills, which were becoming quite large. Jason agreed to give Callie up, though only on paper. Finally, Callie got to come home from the hospital. It was an exciting day—for everyone except Jason. He was told he could no longer see his daughter because he was not good father material—he was seventeen and unemployed.

Lost and miserable, he went to an attorney who was no help. In fact, the attorney also told Jason he would not make a good father. Jason was starting to believe he wasn't good enough for his own daughter. Arranging sneaky visits with Callie's mother to see the baby made him feel even more worthless.

Jason eventually got a job and tried to move forward. Unfortunately, he lost three of his good friends within just a few months. One died in an car accident, one drowned, and another took his life. One morning not long after that, Jason sat alone in his bedroom holding a gun to his head. No one heard the shot that took his life, just as no one heard his cries for help.

Jason called his Aunt Lori shortly before he took his life. He asked her why God took his friends and not him. Lori cries now knowing Jason is with God and with his buddies. But she also smiles, because he is finally happy. No more running away. No more hiding, just peace.

Jason Dean Andresen
Nineteen years old

Dearest Jason,

Hi, sweetheart. Have I told you lately how much I love you? How much I miss you? Have I told you I think of you whenever I see a smile like yours, a truck like yours, beautiful blue eyes like yours, the sun, the moon, the rain? Or how I think of you when I'm at home alone or when someone is with me? When I'm at work or at play (yes, I'm trying to learn how to play again), when I am driving or just walking, sitting, or standing? Always.

You mean everything to me. I miss you, Jason. The way you smiled, the way you laughed. I miss your hugs and your kisses. I miss the silly things you used to say to make me laugh and the crooked little grin you'd give me when you knew you were in trouble.

I don't know why, but there was always something special between us, and I will always be grateful for that. I just wish we had more time together. Sometimes I think I understand why you committed suicide, Jason, but it hurts so much that you're not here. I wish I could go back in time and fix everything for you. You had so much pain in your young life, but you tried so hard. Seeing the pain in your eyes was more than I could bear.

You know, Jason, I never thought this would happen, your dying. My heart has been ripped out, and the pain will never truly go away. When I think about you, sitting in your room preparing yourself for this, I die inside. Why didn't you call me?

When I think about the amount of pain you were in to have done this, I am so mad at myself. Why didn't I realize it was getting that far out of control? You even tried to tell me, and I still didn't get it. I am so sorry, Jason, so very sorry. I'm sorry you had to feel like that. I'm sorry I couldn't make it better.

My memories will always keep you alive, but Lord, Jason, I wish I had more. More time, more chances, more you. More opportunities to see you smile, to hear you laugh, to hold you in my arms and tell you I love you. More chances to help you realize your hopes and dreams, because I know you had them, Jason; you told me about them.

Here I am, writing you this letter, with all the things I wish I could tell you in person. Don't forget me, Jason. I'll never forget you. Someday I'll get to see you again, and when that day comes, I know happiness will overshadow the anguish I've felt at losing you. I love you, buddy, with all my heart.

Aunt Lori

Dawn's Sunrise

She wanted her thirtieth birthday to be one she would never forget. And she wanted to celebrate with a girls only, one-of-a-kind party. The night started with dinner at a four-star restaurant, where the women ate, talked, and laughed. The high energy moved with them from dinner to the theater. Then they capped things off with a limousine ride to Tiffanie's favorite night club.

"Happy Birthday, Dear Tiffanie" was the song of choice. The dressed-up ladies danced their way into the early-morning hours, sharing special times with a friend who helped them sing a little louder, dance a little wilder, and love a lot more deeply.

Tiffanie had a young spirit that enveloped those close to her. She made sure there were no frowns in the crowd, and if one showed up, she did her best to change it into a smile.

Tiffanie's sister-in-law, Dawn, longed for just a small part of Tiffanie's personal power. Tiffanie was her hero. Dawn admired her because she put her heart into everything she did. She made every moment a memory and turned everything into an event.

Before meeting Tiffanie, Dawn believed the glass was half empty. But Tiffanie encouraged her to look toward the future and to find inner strength in faith and prayer. One March evening, however, Tiffanie lost her faith. The newly divorced mother of four ended her life.

Dawn didn't know it then, but that one-of-a-kind thirtieth birthday celebration just a few months before would be the last birthday she and Tiffanie would ever celebrate together. Now Dawn silently wishes her sister-in-law "Happy Birthday," and smiles when she remembers their girls' night out.

Tiffanie Lee Demo
Thirty years old

Dear Tiffanie,

I have thought about you every day since you've been gone. Now that it's been over a year, the thoughts are no longer all angry. They are sometimes mixed with laughter and happy memories of the bond we once shared. You were such an inspiration. I was always glad to say we were related. We were not alike in any other way, other than we both bore four children and we both loved your brother, in one way or another.

It is still so very hard for me to accept the fact that life was too hard for you. I still wonder what the final point of no return was. Didn't you look to the future? You so often told me that things would always get better. Did you really believe that? When you took your last breath, did your children's faces appear over and over?

I feel so selfish. I needed you. Did I need you too much? We talked about everything. Why couldn't you tell me you felt this way? When I think about your last day, I still have a hard time believing you actually meant to die. Maybe you just fell asleep, and your car just happened to be on, and you didn't actually mean to die. When I work through all of this anger, I will eventually think of things I can do in remembrance of you.

I still have your phone number programmed into my phone and still have you on my buddy list and on my mailing list. They will stay there forever. I am not in any rush to delete you. I developed those twenty rolls of film you left in a bowl at your house, and someday I plan to give them to your mom. It will be very hard on her.

I wish so much that I could take all of your mom's pain away. I could never fathom losing a child, especially losing one the way you died. Your kids are such a blessing to your mom. She talks about them all the time. Without her grandchildren, she would have given up when you died. They say that every mom has a child who is most like her. For your mom, that was you. She has been strong through all of this, even though it's a lot for show.

You were my strength. I am sorry I depended too much on you. I never knew that you, too, were struggling. I would have offered my shoulder to you; then we both would have been stronger. I forgive you for leaving us early. I promise I will stay strong for my family, and I'll try very hard to never give up.

I have your pictures everywhere in my house, all the pictures that I could find. I just wish I had put them there before you died. Then maybe you would have known just how very much you are loved and how much you will be missed.

Dawn

A Teen's Insight

As freshman year nears its end, I am busy with papers, presentations, and moving plans. However, today demands that I pause to sit and reflect, along with many of my loved ones. Today we mourn the loss of our beloved Jason, my cousin, my blood, but most importantly, my friend. Jason has been gone from us physically for two years now. But he remains in our thoughts and in our hearts as a guardian angel to us all.

I learned quite a few lessons when Jason died. I later took those lessons and put them in writing for a class paper. I did this because my aunt, who never asks anything of me, made a request: "Tell people about Jason. Do not let his death be for nothing."

The time has come for me to remind people of the priceless life lessons we learn. Aunt Brenda, this is for you, so that others may hopefully never have to experience this grief.

1. Value your time with your loved ones.

I had never been to my maternal grandmother's grave, but my mom and I were near there when we were headed home from a road trip with my youth choir. So, we paid my grandmother a visit. Mom and I talked about death and what we wanted when we died.

The concept of knowing what I wanted for my family after I was gone boggled my mind. I was too young to even think about death. After all, I was only seventeen. People die when they are old and have experienced all life has to offer. Little did I know, I was about to learn my first lesson in heartache.

When we got home everything seemed normal. My dogs jumped and barked, and dinner was on the stove. I looked out the back window and saw my father in the yard on the phone. After he hung up, he came inside, upset. I asked who was on the phone. And that's when he told me.

"Jason is dead."

My cousin, Jason, was only twenty-five. He was my favorite aunt's son, and he had a twin brother named Ricky. The twins and I were the Three Musketeers. I would visit them in Panama City at least once a year. The three of us would watch movies, go to the beach, and do mischievous things our parents would not want us to do.

I never expected to lose Jason. I had never thought about losing anyone I loved. I wish I could go back in time and memorize every moment we had together. I know now to value the time we have with loved ones, because we never know how much time we have left with them.

2. It is never too late.

Jason died on a Sunday. His funeral was the following Thursday. Everyone close to Jason came. The focus was on mourning my cousin, but we were also thinking about my father and paternal grandfather. They had not spoken in twenty years. My father was a pallbearer and my grandfather sang during the service, yet each kept to his respective corner. When the time came to leave, an amazing thing happened. My grandfather walked up to my father, and they hugged.

That hug taught me that hope exists even in death. Jason would have loved to have seen what happened. Oh, I also learned it is never too late to call a truce.

3. Learn to cope.

Learning to cope with the death of a loved one is very difficult. After I recovered from the initial shock, I became very angry with Jason. How could he do that to his family? Worse, my Aunt Brenda had to bury one of her sons on the Thursday before Mother's Day. I was enraged. After awhile, though, I started to realize that maybe Jason did not know he was going to affect our family as much as he did. I am no longer mad at him, but I still get distressed about his death.

My family as a whole, my aunt, and my life will never be the same. I learned to move on by realizing that even though Jason is dead, he will live on in my heart, and I can still love him.

4. Life is short.

Life flies by, and what seems like a moment, in reality is two years. As I think of everything that has happened in the past two years, I wonder if I am living my life fully. Would I be satisfied with the way I have lived if I were to die tomorrow? Would Jason be proud of me?

Since Jason died, I have danced, sung, cried, swum in the ocean, and skied on mountain tops; but most importantly, I have matured and learned to value every day, no matter what it holds.

Live for the moment, as if you are going to die tomorrow. Life is too short to try to live it to please others. Live your life for yourself, but be full of love and respect.

5. Remember where you came from.

Always remember your family and what they have done for you. These are the special friends who leave footprints on our hearts. I have learned to be thankful for all that people have done for me, and the person they have helped me become. We would not be who we are without our families.

6. Don't look back.

How can we possibly see what lies ahead if we are stuck looking back? "What ifs" and "if onlys" do not matter. Do not live with regret for mistakes, but instead, embrace what can be learned from them. Look toward tomorrow and all the hope and joy it holds. That does not mean to forget the past; it means to not let memories bring you sorrow.

7. Live, love, and remember.

It's as simple as that. Keep in touch with loved ones. Never let a day go by that you do not think of them and remember them in your prayers. Today, as I walked to class, I paused. It was just for a moment, but that single moment held so much. I closed my eyes, tilted my head as the sun shone on my face, breathed, and felt the warm embrace of love no longer here, but still very much alive.

Please do not let my cousin's death be for nothing. Learn from the pain and grief my family has endured, and do not bring this grief to those you hold dear.

Leslie A. DeLuna
Jason's Cousin

Jason Lee Grubbs
Twenty-five years old

Jason was a cocaine addict. Not long before he died, he called his mother's home and talked to his stepfather, Tommy. Jason told him he wanted to stop hurting his mother. His last words to Tommy were, "Tell Mom I love her."

Jason's mom wrote the following words shortly after his death. They can now be said to Jason's twin brother, Rick, as well. He suicided while this book was being written.

I saw you today not with my eyes, with my mind.
    I hugged you today not with my arms, with my heart.
I heard you whisper, "Mommy," not in my ears, through the wind.
    My ears heard the thunder crack.
My heart feels the impact.
    My mind understands
Why you decided to go.
    My heart refuses to believe it was so.
I saw you today not with my eyes, with my mind.
    I hugged you today not with my arms, with my heart.
I told you I love you today not in words, with longing.

Brenda Adkins
Mother to Jason and Rick

Rocky Mountain Memory

Although it happened twenty years ago, I remember it like it was yesterday. It was October. My phone rang. Kelly was on the line, and what she was about to say would forever change so many lives.

I had only been at Texas Tech since the start of the fall semester, and I was homesick for the kids I used to teach at Aurora Christian Academy in Colorado, especially my cheerleaders. We spent most of that summer together at cheerleading camp and practices. I had grown to love each of them.

Now in Texas, I looked forward to their calls about the latest football game, their newest boyfriends, and the campus gossip. But something was alarmingly different about Kelly's voice that night.

"It's not good news. Tynele shot herself. She's dead."

Grief slammed me like a hammer, crushing me in a swift cruel moment; all the breath was wrenched from my body. Her words reverberated in my head, growing louder and louder, tearing into my soul. Kelly and I were both crying. Then she explained as best she could what had happened, but the details didn't matter. What I couldn't accept was that something depressed Tynele so much that she pulled the trigger. What went through her mind at that very moment?

I felt suspended, as if watching a play slowly unfold on stage. Tynele dead? No! When I left for Texas Tech, she was laughing and crying and teasing me about being a college woman once again. We promised to talk every week and see each other at Thanksgiving. That was just a few weeks away.

I felt responsible, as if my staying in Colorado would have prevented her from ending her life. If I'd been there, we could have talked; I could have helped her through her pain. I wanted to scream and disappear forever.

I had to tell my eight-year-old son, Jason, although I knew I would never be able to help him fully understand why his favorite baby-sitter chose death over life. I picked him up at school, and, as gently as possible, I told him. His face went blank. He didn't cry. He was simply speechless. We drove around for hours; I was crying, Jason was staring out the window. When we got home, he slammed the door and kicked the car. I knew how he felt.

One of my most vivid memories of Tynele is from cheerleading camp. I came back from a coach's meeting and the girls were in a circle with their backs to each other, refusing to talk. Knowing how very stubborn each of them was, I was worried, especially when Kelly told me they all just wanted to go home.

My job was to teach them that persistence and determination were two of the most important traits a person could learn. They all listened and decided to give their friendship and the competition their best shot. Even Tynele. When they won first place, we all cried. I was so proud of them.

I will never know the pain Tynele had right before she put the gun to her head. I wish she could have pushed those thoughts aside and thought back to that day at camp with her friends—the day they decided they could get through whatever problems they had and come out on top. I wish Tynele had heeded that lesson one more time.

Belita Nelson
Tynele's Friend

Tynele Rene Fincher
Fifteen years old

Dear Tynele,

I am writing to tell you how much I love you and how much I miss you. So many friends loved you deeply, and your family cared more than you knew. I worried about your mom and dad and wondered what I could possibly say to them.

I want you to know I am no longer mad at you. It took months of therapy and years of contemplation to dissolve my anger. But I still suffer from incredible sadness that the world was cheated by the absence of your incredible spirit.

I wonder what your life could have been. I remember your infectious laughter and incredible sense of humor and how you made us laugh when everything was tense. Your eyes sparkled, even when you were angry. And your red hair! You did have a temper to match that hair, but your anger would dissipate as quickly as it flared. I wonder who you would have married and what your children would have been like.

Time makes us wiser, and now I understand some things. God provided us a gift, a power so incredible that most of us ignore it, because it is far too challenging for us to comprehend. That gift is the power of choice. I don't understand it, but I accept that you were using your power of choice. Each and every day we must make choices. You made yours.

Tynele, you influenced me in an incredible manner. Your death, even though I failed to realize it at the time, set me on a course of creating my own destiny. I was teaching in Plano, Texas, when our community faced a rash of heroin addiction in students. Jason, my son, the boy you babysat, was one of those kids. This time, I got mad. I channeled my anger into creating the Starfish Foundation, a nonprofit organization dedicated to providing a venue to listen to those crying out.

We help parents who have nowhere else to turn. We provide real-world education to teens on the dangers of experimentation. We've even written a program designed to improve substance abuse treatment and increase treatment efficiency.

I've come full circle. Suicide, depression, alcoholism, drug addiction—this is the world I've chosen to influence. If we save one life, we've made a difference. I wish I could have saved yours. Thank you for the lessons I learned from your life and your death.

I love you,

Belita

Help to Heal a Friend's Heart

If someone you know, either casually or intimately, has suicided, you are not alone. Every day in this country, mothers and fathers, daughters and sons, sisters and brothers, and friends and lovers end their lives.

If this person was an acquaintance, you were probably shocked to hear the news. "What happened? Is it true? Is he really gone?" If the person was someone close, those feelings may be compounded with tremendous guilt: "Why didn't I see it coming? Why didn't I do something to prevent it?" (see "Soul Sisters").

The suicide of a friend brings feelings of sadness, grief, and loss. We feel helpless and confused, and we wonder how this could have happened. Sometimes we feel angry with our friend for leaving us, especially since we are unprepared to deal with his or her sudden death (see "The War and the Wall"). Often, we then feel even more guilt because we are being selfish and only thinking of our loss. The suicide of someone we know brings conflicting feelings unlike any other unexpected death. We must work through all these feelings to put what happened in perspective (see "Dawn's Sunrise").

The death of a friend is often perceived as less of a loss than that of a family member, even though the friendship might have been extremely close. If the individual was a best friend, you might have been closer to him or her than to your immediate family. However, friends seldom receive the same support as family members after a death.

You might not be involved in the planning of the funeral or memorial service. You might receive less support from helping professionals, like doctors and nurses, funeral directors, or memorial planners. You might feel like you don't have a place in your friend's life anymore, and that your friendship wasn't important to other people or to the friend's family.

You won't be eligible for any time off from work. You might not even be able to go to the funeral if it's out of your city. These issues can lead to isolation in your grief at a time when you need support from someone who understands.

Here are some things you can do to help get through this difficult time:

1. Find someone you can trust, and talk it out.

A minister, priest, rabbi, or other spiritual counselor will listen to you and keep your thoughts confidential. A trained psychotherapist, especially one who specializes in grief and loss issues, can also be of great help. Your friends probably won't be able to hear you talk out your feelings for as long as it takes to recover, so look for a professional who is trained to listen.

2. Start a journal to sort out your feelings.

It's free, available, and confidential. Studies show that those who write out their feelings recover quicker, experience less stress-related illness, and attain a better quality of life than those who don't journal. Writing about feelings is even shown to be as effective as talking to a therapist for some people. Journaling is one of the best tools you can use to help with your recovery. You can see examples of journaling in the letters, poems, and journal entries throughout this book. There is a place near the end of the book for you to journal your thoughts.

3. Locate suicide survivor groups.

Most cities have a suicide crisis center, and these centers often conduct survivor support groups. These groups can be of immense help. You will receive support from those who have experienced the same type of loss but are further along in the grieving process than you are.

If you go to the meetings, you will meet people who are at the same place in the process which will help you see your feelings as normal. After attending for a while, you will recognize, by hearing what the new members are saying, how much you have worked through your own grief, and you will realize that your feelings are no longer quite so raw and intense.

There are also online groups and crisis hotlines you can reach out to. You can find a reference list of helpful phone numbers and Web sites in the back of this book.

4. Educate yourself about the stages of grief.

Learn about the grieving stages to help you understand the process of loss—whether it's through death, divorce, job loss, loss of a loved pet, or even moving to another location. The stages are denial, anger, bargaining, depression, and acceptance. Be patient with yourself in getting through these stages. Grief is a process that takes time. Give yourself that time, go slowly, and show yourself the same loving patience you would show a friend.

5. Recognize that grief is one of the great equalizers of life.

Precious few of us get through life without some devastating losses, yet we survive and grow. We often love again. We become stronger, more compassionate, more understanding, less judgmental, and more mature. We get through tough times. We learn how to cope with change, the only constant in life.

6. Give yourself the gift of support.

Make the loss of your friend count for something positive (see "Rocky Mountain Memory"). You will never be the same after going through the suicide of a friend or loved one. You can get through it, and the changes in you may well result in helping others throughout the rest of your life. What better way to honor and memorialize the life of someone you love?

I wish you peace in your journey toward healing.

Diane Weatherford, MEd, LPC[1]

---

1. Diane Weatherford has worked for nonprofit counseling/crisis centers for more than fifteen years. She has also served as the executive director of the Dallas Fort Worth nonprofit organization, CONTACT Counseling and Crisis Line. Her primary fields of focus include chemical dependence, substance abuse, and relationship issues.

Journey of One
Loves Left Behind

"How Long"

Nights alone for me
       Now that you're gone
Spent wishing on stars
       From dusk until dawn

I know you hear me
       The wishes I've tried
One star to the next
       My wish is denied

—Wade Hendricks
Songwriter

Goodnight Moon

Never in her worst nightmare did Susan Greenwood see it coming, especially since it started as such a beautiful dream. She was only nineteen when she first saw Gary Bloy's boyish dimples. Their flirting turned to infatuation, and their first kiss turned to the promise of forever.

But Susan's parents didn't like Gary. They had heard enough gossip about him in their small Wisconsin town to know they did not want him in their daughter's life. Her parents' disapproval only made the rebellious Susan more attracted to Gary.

Gary showered Susan with attention; he gave her flowers, candy, and cards. They went on camping, ice fishing, and hunting trips. But the longer they dated, the more selfish he became with her time. He did not want to share her with anyone, not even family or friends. He made sure she was isolated, even taking her to dinner in restaurants more than an hour's drive from their home. Back then, Susan didn't see his behavior as controlling. She does now.

Whenever Susan thinks about how happy they were in the beginning, she cries. She cries for what was and what can never be. She also cries because those memories are so different from the ones made after they were married. That's when Gary's love turned to obsession. He wanted to know where she was and whom she was with at all times. If she went on a walk through the neighborhood, he knew how long it should take, and if she was even a few minutes off from his time table, he would accuse her of being unfaithful.

When she talked on the phone, he would get angry that he was not getting attention. So without even realizing she was doing it, she pulled away from family and friends. If she wasn't there when and where Gary wanted her to be, there would be a price to pay—verbally, emotionally, and in the end, physically.

Susan thought things would get better after the children were born. She was wrong. Gary emotionally abandoned the family, except to take his anger out on Susan. There was jealousy, rage, and daily degrading. He even denied that their youngest child, Elizabeth, was his and refused to touch her until she was several months old.

Gary's drinking was getting worse and so was the domination. Slapping, shoving, and spitting were his ways of communicating. Susan's sense of self-worth was nonexistent. She didn't have the courage to leave until she believed her children were in danger.

Like everything else in the household, Gary controlled the money. So with barely more than the clothes they wore, Susan and her three children went to a shelter. They stayed there for four months. When Gary found out they moved to a place of their own, he was outraged. The anger boiled over one hot August night.

Gary torched the home he and Susan once shared. Clothing, books, pictures, toys, dishes, furniture—nothing was spared. The smoke and fire carried the memories off into the night air. He then got into his car and left the burning home behind. As he drove those dark and quiet country roads, Susan and her young daughter were across town reading bedtime stories on the sofa. The two boys were sleeping in their bedrooms.

Just as firefighters arrived at Gary's home in another part of town, Susan and Elizabeth heard someone breaking in. They sat there, still and silent. Seconds later, the man Susan fell in love with as a teenager stood in front of them, with a gun. No one said anything, not even Gary. He just made some sort of screaming sound.

Elizabeth yelled, "No, Daddy, no!"

Her voice brought him out of whatever state of mind he was in. He slowly made eye contact with them and then left as quickly as he came. He rushed past his toddler son, Ramsey, who was crying in the hallway. He ran to the backyard, put the gun in his mouth, and pulled the trigger.

Susan and her children are now trying to recover, both emotionally and financially. They were left with broken hearts and only twenty-six dollars. But for Susan, her children's safety is all that matters. She has finally woken up from her nightmare and now faces the nightmares of her children. She hopes one day they can wake up, too, but she's afraid they never will.

Gary Alan Bloy
Thirty-seven years old

> Gary,
>
> Not a single day passes that doesn't include thoughts of you—thoughts that range from when you were almost a decent husband, to the awful monster you became. My emotions for you run the entire spectrum. But the strongest emotion is fear—fear of what you could have done, and fear of the things you tried to do to our children, my family, and me.
>
> My hate and anger toward you are pacified by my guilt. Yes, Gary, you did it again. You succeeded in making me feel responsible for your actions. People have done their best to assure me it wasn't my fault. I've read books that tell me I'm not responsible. I guess in my head I know it's not my fault. Funny, I've yet to convince my heart of that.
>
> You have done things to me that made me an emotional basket case. I'm still afraid of you with the same intense measure of terror as when you put that gun in my face. Yet among the emotions is a four-letter word that very few people believe I can feel for you. Love.

Gary, how could you not know I loved you? I still, in an odd way, love you. Couldn't you feel it the times I believed your promises that you'd change? Couldn't you feel it when I cried for you to get help?

I have to keep it together now, Gary, because I am a mother to our three children. Remember them? Yes, the kids you left devastated and traumatized. Your obituary said you were a loving father. Whatever! What kind of man leaves his kids without a dad? You were a coward, a selfish, rotten human being. I can say that, because I am the one who had to tell the kids you were dead. I had to answer the questions and calm their fears. I had to get your face put back together so they could say goodbye. I have to be there when the nightmares come. They are so confused.

Hunter's afraid of being like you. He is an awesome student and a brilliant reader. He's got glasses, you know. Hunter just wants to be liked, and your rejection and abandonment have him troubled.

Elizabeth can't admit what she saw, because it would kill her to accept it. But she is one tough chick. She has to be to hide her sadness and fear. I'm thinking ten more years of therapy will help her out. She went to her first father-daughter dance. She looked precious. Pink, silk long skirt, hat, gloves, and a little lipstick. It was a long night explaining why her godfather, Uncle Paul, was there and not you.

Ramsey doesn't remember anything, but he knows all his preschool buddies have dads. I guess he's the lucky one. He escaped your nightmare without any huge scars. You can't miss what you've never had.

It could've been worked out. You should have gotten help. But you didn't. You lose. I wish you wouldn't have made us lose, too.

As Always,

Susan

Susan's children and sister wrote letters to Gary. You can find those letters in "Children Left Behind" and "Friends Left Behind."

Nazarene Water Truck

Jim and Linda just finished planning a trip to the lake. They couldn't wait to pack up their RV and get out of Dallas for a few days. They wanted to catch fish, sit by a crackling fire, and enjoy the sounds of crickets singing them to sleep.

Satisfied everything would go as planned, the couple sat down to watch the evening news. The deadly tornadoes in Oklahoma City led the newscast. Winds up to 318 mph ripped across Oklahoma, killing dozens of people and leaving behind more than 1.5 billion dollars in damage.

Before the report was over, Jim and Linda had changed their fishing plans. They still loaded up the RV and put their beat-up black pickup truck on the tow dolly, but instead of looking for fish, they looked for tornado victims. Their journey took them to a Nazarene Church in Midwest City to a relief center.

Linda and Jim walked into the fellowship hall where he humbly said, "We're the McKees from Texas, and we're here to help. What can we do?"

Jim and Linda gave their neighbors to the north a hand to hold and a shoulder to cry on. Both nurses, they also provided medical care, as well as prayer and counseling. But most of the time, Jim and Linda drove around in that old black truck of theirs, passing out water, sunscreen, bandages, and whatever else they had on hand. Town folk christened that black pickup the "Nazarene Water Truck."

After they got back to Texas, Jim's health grew progressively worse, and he fell into a deep depression. He suffered a slight stroke, but his primary physical problem was peripheral neuropathy. He described the pain to Linda as electric shocks up and down his legs. That pain also went into his arms. Not a day went by that he wasn't in pain.

Before Jim got ill, he and Linda traveled the US and Africa, spreading Christianity. They taught from the Bible and from their hearts. It was their calling. In the States, Jim helped build a sanctuary for a Nazarene Church in Pilot Point, Texas. That church is now used to train pastors for the Church of the Nazarene.

During a journey to Africa, Jim worked with a refugee camp in Swaziland. He bought prenatal vitamins and worm medicine for the refugees. He then set up a pill distribution system for them.

Jim always wanted to go back to Africa. But after he got sick, he quickly went from using one cane to two. Then he went from a walker to a wheelchair. He knew he could never go back. That thought killed him long before the gunshot wound ever did.

The day Jim took his life, the shot was heard around the world. It was heard in Africa by those who are alive and healthy because of him. It was heard in Pilot Point by those who have a sanctuary to pray in because of him. And it was heard in Oklahoma by those who needed a friend after the tornadoes.

Thomas James "Jim" McKee

Fifty-eight years old

> Dearest Jim,
>
> I'll always remember the evening you walked back into my life. I can still see you stepping up the driveway in your black leather coat with that big smile that always made my heart flutter. That's where I go whenever the movie starts rolling

in my head, when I see that terrible night that you shot yourself.

Those images don't overwhelm me like they used to, but they haven't gone away. They probably never will. Your last words still haunt me. "You won't ever have to worry about me again. And you won't have a mess to clean up, either."

You cocked the shotgun, walked down the hall into the bathroom, and closed the door. The shot was so loud and the stillness afterward, even louder. The 911 operator told me not to open the door, but I had to. I couldn't believe what had just happened. When I saw you, I knew you were dead.

You didn't really get rid of your pain, you know; you just passed it on to me. I believe you thought you were doing me a favor by killing yourself. You thought taking care of you was a burden for me. Yes, you were in pain every day, but the pain your dignity suffered was greater than your physical pain. I saw that whenever I loaded the wheelchair into the trunk. I could see the sadness in your eyes because I had to do so much for you.

Every time you looked out into the driveway, you saw the RV that you would never be able to drive again. I sold the RV. I couldn't bear the thought of going anyplace in it without you. You wrapped yourself up in everything you couldn't do any longer. Why didn't you ever see all that you could still do?

I know you are in heaven and that you have a whole body again. I hope you now know how many people loved you and how many lives you touched. I'll always treasure our good times. You are the love of my life.

Linda

From Malta with Love

Theirs was the type of love most think exists only on the silver screen: exploding fireworks, butterflies in your stomach, ringing bells when you kiss. But the love between AnnMarie and Ray wasn't made in Hollywood. This love story happened on the streets of Malta.

Ray was sixteen years her senior, but their love was ageless. Both professional violists with the Malta National Symphony Orchestra, they traveled, performed, loved, and laughed, spending every waking and sleeping moment at each other's side. Still, that was not enough time.

Their passion lasted a little more than a year. During that time, Ray hid the fact that he was bipolar. Finally, he could hide it no more. In the last three weeks of his life, Ray tried to suicide eight times. Each time, AnnMarie saved him. But the ninth time, love couldn't save him.

Now AnnMarie plays in the orchestra without Ray. She stares at his chair, occupied by another violist. Still, the music plays on. So perhaps theirs was a story written in Hollywood—a screenplay with a tragic ending, where true loves are left broken-hearted, with nothing more than precious memories to comfort their aching souls.

Raymond Abela
Forty-three years old

> Dear Ray,
>
> It's difficult to accept reality without questioning it. It is much easier to say, "If only." If only we could live forever, if only we could run away from the truth, break down the walls that

keep us apart, be together, forget the sadness, and escape the pain. After accepting the pain and absorbing the tragedy, what I have found is you.

We were given the gift of a lifetime—one last chance to love and be loved. There were no limitations of love, no walls, no boundaries. Our love made us free, complete. Now our time here is up. I'm trying to smile through my tears. I'll try to go on and keep you with me, deep in my heart.

I'll look back without turning back and remember the love we shared. You will be the radiance in my smile, the music in my eyes. You'll always be my strength, my hope, and the most precious gift of my lifetime.

From me to you, my immortal beloved,

AnnMarie

Something Blue

She was only seventeen when her first child was born. Being pregnant in high school was not what the honor student expected. She was supposed to go to college and make a better life. That was her destiny.

Linda Kelly's destiny changed the day she found her mother hanging from the garage rafters by an extension cord. Linda's father could not bear to walk into the garage after that, so he and Linda packed up and moved away. But nothing changed except the scenery. Linda was still sad and lonely. Her father was still emotionally unavailable.

When Tony walked into her life, he seemed to fill every need the young girl had, emotionally, spiritually, and sexually. Linda and Tony became pregnant during their senior year. They were in love and thought they could make it work.

They were married in a wonderful ceremony, surrounded by loving family and friends. But the absence of Linda's mother was a dark cloud that hung over her that April day. On the outside she was smiling; on the inside her heart was breaking. She wanted her mom there, fixing her veil and giving her last-minute words of wisdom.

Following tradition, Linda carried something old, new, borrowed, and blue. Her "old" was an heirloom piece of family jewelry. Her "new" was her white lace gown. And for her "borrowed" item, a friend lent Linda a pair of pearl earrings. Linda did not need anything tangible for something "blue"; she held that in her soul. That emptiness had been there since her mother's death.

Linda and Tony settled down for what they hoped would be a happy life. He went to work for her father at a bakery, and she began her responsibilities as a wife and mother. They were a hard-working, loving family, but Tony began drinking when financial and child-rearing issues became too hard to handle. They were so young when they married, and Linda often thought Tony wasn't ready for his new life. But she stood by him, willing to wait out his confusion.

In just a few short years, Linda gave birth to two more children. Tony began to drink more, leaving her home alone with their three children. The weight of keeping house and home became too much for her. Their once loving relationship turned into a roller-coaster ride. He would drink; she would leave. He would sober up; she would come back. But finally, she had had enough and left for good. Linda never stopped loving Tony. She still wanted to be his wife. She just needed him to be there for their family.

Hung over or not, Tony never missed work. So when he didn't show up that August day, Linda's dad called and said he was worried. When Linda called Tony's home, a police officer answered. Linda was thrown back to the day she found her mother's body. She knew something was very wrong then, and she had that same feeling now.

Barely getting the question out, Linda screamed, "Is he dead?"

The officer replied quietly, "I'm sorry."

Linda continued screaming as she ran out the front door. Her firstborn, Ray, who was three, looked out the window and watched his mother have a breakdown in their yard. Ray and Linda seldom talked about that day, but neither forgot it.

Tony shot himself in the head, and Linda once again found herself grieving a loved one lost to suicide. Just as she did when her mother died, Linda packed up her family to start a new life. She was just twenty-one and a widow, with three children under the age of three.

The deaths of Linda's mother and husband were two of three great tragedies she would suffer. Years later, her son, Ray, would become the third.

Anthony "Tony" Dale Webb
Twenty-four years old

Dear Tony,

I miss you so much. I am so sorry that you left. I wish you had held on. Maybe we could have worked things out. You missed so much with the kids. They really needed you. I am not mad, though. Please don't think that. You must have been very depressed, and I didn't realize it. I wish I could have done things differently. Please forgive me.

I love you, Tony, and always will. Please keep our son safe. I pray that Mom, you, and Ray will greet me at heaven's gates when I leave this place. I pray for you every day, Tony. I will always love you, sweetheart.

Linda

You can find other stories about Linda and her family in "Children Left Behind" and "Parents Left Behind."

Rebel with a Cause

Looking like he just stepped off a movie set, Dave wore tight, faded blue jeans and hiking boots with cracks and creases where wind and weather bit hard into them. His blonde feathered hair framed his chiseled tanned face. Those devilishly handsome good looks grabbed Tracy's heart.

But Tracy fell in love with the person beneath the rugged outdoorsman. Dave was kind and giving, caring and understanding, yet he also had a quiet sadness. He didn't talk about it often, but that sadness ultimately led to his death.

The couple lived in Wisconsin, spending cold winters sledding and warm summers riding motorcycles. They were very much in love, but after eight years together, Tracy wanted more. She wanted marriage and a family. Since Dave did not want to walk down the aisle, Tracy decided to walk alone for awhile.

Tracy held out hope for their future together, but she still moved forward with her own life, graduating from college and starting a career. Dave, however, stood still. Life without Tracy was not what he wanted; nor did he want the memories of what he had seen ten years earlier. That's when Dave found his younger brother, Richard, hanging from a tree in the family backyard—the yard of the home Dave still lived in.

Dave rarely talked about Richard, but when he did, a deep emptiness filled his voice. He missed his brother desperately. Tracy was the only person Dave opened up to about Richard. Not even his family understood what he went through after finding Richard's lifeless body. Without Tracy, Dave felt even more lost and alone.

Dave told a friend how desperate he was and that he was considering suicide. His friend made him promise he would never do such a thing. Dave promised. He also lied.

Dave woke up that Friday morning and got ready for work. He said good-bye to his dad and drove away. He left work early that day, stopped for fast food, and then drove home. He parked near the back of the house, close to the same tree where his brother hung himself. Dave ate his food, then picked up the gun he purchased just two days before and shot himself.

Tracy repeatedly called Dave that night. She had a feeling something was wrong. He did not return her calls. Saturday passed, then Sunday morning. That's when two officers stood at her front door and told her what happened. Dave had been dead forty-eight hours. Only after her calls to his parents did anyone look in his truck.

Tracy no longer has dreams of a life with Dave. She now has nightmares about how he left this world and what he is missing. No more motorcycle rides to Whitnall Park. No more swimming in the Wisconsin Dells.

Dave is gone, and Tracy has only the memories of the man with the beautiful face and even more beautiful spirit. Her movie star. Her hero. Her Dave.

David Michael Klingler
Twenty-nine years old

Dear Dave,
> I woke up this morning and thought of you. It is going to be a beautiful day outside—sunny and eighty-five degrees. You would love to be riding your motorcycle today.

I really miss you and think of you all the time. I think about the good times we shared together, but I am still very upset about what you did. You're missing out on so many things: Miller Park, the Packers at Lambeau Field, new food at fast-food restaurants, flying in an airplane, and just being alive.

I miss calling you and telling you about my day at work. I miss you holding me. Sometimes I am so angry with you, and then sometimes I miss you more than words can say. What hurts me the most is that you were in so much pain, and I didn't even know it. I would have done anything to help you. I love you so much! I hope that you are in a better place and not hurting anymore. I also hope that you find your brother.

I'm sure you know that I put a really nice wind chime in the tree next to your grave. Whenever I visit, I hear the soft chimes playing music from the wind. It makes me feel as if you're close to me. I also have the same wind chime hanging in my living room. I just wish that it would chime without the wind blowing, to give me a sign that you're looking over me.

I'll always love you,

Tracy

Leaving Las Vegas

It's a place where love and loot are lost, and where forever and fortunes are found. For Phil and Tishia, it was all that and more. He was near the end of his life. She was near the beginning of hers. But for a few short years, this pair took a chance on love and won.

The tall, handsome Jersey son was born into America's Roaring Twenties. The country was kicking up its heels, dancing and drinking to the tune of prosperity. The light-haired, blue-eyed Italian had a taste for fine living and dining. He owned small restaurants for years until he opened the one that made it big. The boy-from-across-the-bridge finally made his mark.

Phil took his fortune to Sin City. The Rat Pack made him feel right at home, and he was soon one of the city's most popular playboys. Decades later, during the Brat Pack era, when Carter, not Coolidge, was in office, Tishia was born. At seventeen, the shy Generation Xer left her California home to make a better life in Las Vegas.

Lady Luck was on Phil's side the day he walked into the brunette beauty's life. She was a nurse's aid and had just started working with Phil's doctor. Phil and Tishia became friends, and she soon began taking care of him at his home, doing what he couldn't do for himself. She helped with physical therapy, medication, errands, and household responsibilities. Neither minded when their friendship took a flirtatious turn, even though there was a fifty-year age difference between them.

Favorite evenings together were made up of playing games, drinking wine, and eating a gourmet meal, cooked by Phil, of course. But as the years went on, Phil's health worsened. He had emphysema, heart problems, and an increasingly painful hernia. Tishia promised to be with him, the man she loved, her best friend, forever.

Eventually, the time came when even standing was too painful for Phil. He loved Tishia and did not want her to waste her youth beside a dying old man. She was the one who found his body. She remembers staring at the man she loves, holding the note he left her. "No tears, kiddo. I love you." That's all he had written.

Three months after Phil died, Tishia left Las Vegas. She went back to her family's home in California. On Phil's birthday, just four months after he ended his pain, Tishia walked down her small town street and released fifty balloons. Inside each balloon was a handwritten note carrying a message of love and hope. The message Tishia has with her today is one of patience, thankful for her time with Phil, knowing they will meet again. Fate brought them together that day at the doctor's office, but it will be fortune that keeps them together when they meet in heaven.

Philip Cintura
Seventy-eight years old

Phil,

Tomorrow will be five months since the day I found you. What a long five months. I have not done what you asked, because to ask for "no tears" was a lot. I can't help but cry when I think of you. I guess I am selfish, but I am not ready to move on without you. I want you with me when I wake up. I want to hear the same stories you told me over and over, and forgot you told me the first time.

You were the reason I breathed each day. You are the reason I can say I have been loved and have loved someone with every ounce of my heart and soul. I may never love like that again, but I don't need to. You gave me what no one else can or will.

I want to be mad at you and scream at the top of my lungs. I want to pretend that this never happened and go back to the life we had. I don't want to make myself sick crying. I have to live each day with the consequences of your decision. I have to live with my pain and sadness without you. I guess your decision was a way out of a life you were tired of living. I just don't understand.

I was always there for you and would have never left your side. We both knew that you did not have much time left. I just thought you would die naturally and that I would be there to hold your hand and tell you I loved you. I didn't think I would find you the way I did. I never thought I would feel every ounce of life leave my body as it did that morning.

I need to know a few things, Phil. I need to know you can hear me right now and that you can see me. I need to know you still know how much I love you and that I would have given you my last breath so you would not hurt anymore. I need to know you are with me and that you will never leave my side.

I want to know it didn't hurt. I want to know your last thoughts. I hope you thought of me. I hope you thought of the great life you lived and the great things you gave people just by being part of their lives.

I want you to know you were the most wonderful thing to ever come into my life. Because of you I am a better person. You will always be the love of my life. I will live forever with you in my heart. If I mess up, just hold my hand and help me through it. If I need a hug, feel free to reach down and touch my heart.

I love you forever,

Tishia Lei

Love's First Loss

In many ways their love story is just like everybody else's. They met, fell in love, and planned a life together. But that's where this couple's story takes a turn. This is the story of Brandi and Monica, as told by Brandi.

Summer break had just ended, and I was proud to be heading back to high school with my beautiful new girlfriend. She was my first girlfriend and I was hers. We were inseparable from the day we met until the day she died.

The beginning of the end started when the unthinkable happened. Monica's brother and some of his friends violently raped her more than once. Monica told me what happened, but she didn't tell anyone else. Keeping that secret caused her an incredible amount of pain, so I encouraged her to talk to her mom. When she finally found the courage to open up, her mother didn't believe her. She said if it really happened, then Monica got what she deserved because of the homosexual lifestyle she had "chosen."

Monica decided to move three hundred miles away to her grandmother's home. Just before she was supposed to leave, she and her mother got into a huge fight. Monica was hysterical and asked me to come over. She told me all she wanted was a home where she felt safe and loved.

I found her crying on her bed. I hugged her and then went to the bathroom to get her a cold cloth. When I got back to her room, she was still sitting there on the bed. Only now she was bleeding. She had cut her wrists. She was bleeding all over the bed and herself. I held her and tried to stop the bleeding. Nothing worked. She died before the ambulance could get there.

I didn't know what to do, what to think, what to feel. I just sat there numb. I was in a nightmare, and all I wanted to do was wake up. Two days after Monica took her life, I couldn't take the pain anymore. I tried to overdose on pills. I realize now that I didn't really want to kill myself. I just wanted someone to tell me everything was going to get better and that the pain would go away.

I was in the hospital for a couple of weeks, but things seemed to get worse when I got back home. I self-mutilated, isolated myself, had nightmares, lost sleep, and didn't care about anything or anyone.

About a year and a half after later, I realized Monica was gone, and I could do nothing to change that. Tired of being miserable, I had to get on with my life. That was the second-hardest thing I have ever done. Holding Monica in my arms as she died was the first.

Everything happens for a reason, even though I may never know the reason why I had to lose Monica. I do not want her death to be in vain. I plan to start working at a suicide crisis center and, hopefully, keep someone from making a huge mistake they can never take back. I am doing this for Monica and for myself.

Brandi Alexander
Monica's Girlfriend

Monica Nicole Byrd

Sixteen years old

Dear Monica,

It's been a little over five years now, and I wanted to write you to tell you what I felt that night and how it's affected me since. When I saw you in your room, I felt like my whole world was crashing in on me. I sat there in your bed with you in my arms until after the ambulance got there. I watched you die and couldn't do anything to stop it.

I felt paralyzed and numb. I hurt so badly inside. I thought things were beginning to get better, since you were going to move away. I guess that wasn't the case. I was so angry with you for not telling me how you really felt. A part of me is gone forever. How could God let something like this happen to you? Why didn't He stop you?

I tried to overdose and almost died. I didn't want to die; I just wanted the pain to stop. After I got out of the hospital, I continued to feel empty and alone. Then one day I woke up and realized you are gone and there is nothing I can do to change that.

I got help and started the long journey to a better and happier life. It's been a slow, rough, and stressful journey, but I am not going to give up. Not a day goes by that I don't think about you or about us. But I know you are in a better place now.

I never went to your funeral because of your family being there. I still don't have a clue where you are buried. I believe you knew I mourned for you and didn't forget you, and that's all that counts. I miss the way you made me a better person. I haven't let many people see the real me since you. I miss being able to open up. Maybe someday we will be able to do that again.

Until then, I have to continue with my life, but that doesn't mean I will forget about you. I will never forget you. I forgive you, and I still love you as much as I did when you were here.

I love you,

Brandi

Unfinished Life

After twelve years of battling alcoholism, my husband, Ken, took his life. Alcohol proved more powerful than we were. It changed him into somebody I didn't want to know. We separated two months before his death. I had no other choice. I had to save our three children and myself. I told Ken we could be a family again after he got help with his anger issues. Sadly, love wasn't enough.

I met Ken shortly after his first suicide attempt. If rescue workers had been ten minutes later, that attempt would have been successful. Successful? That's not a good word. Success to me should be reserved for something positive.

I really can't tell you much about Ken's childhood or what his life was like before me. He didn't like talking about it. It took a lot for him to open up to anyone, and I feel honored that, as his wife and best friend, he did reveal some of his deepest thoughts to me. That included growing up with an abusive father. Ken took a lot of beatings, and so did his mother.

Ken's mother finally left his father, and she did her best to raise her children, taking whatever minimum-wage job she could find. She also got government assistance. Money was tight, so they usually ate bologna or spaghetti, whatever was cheap and would go far enough to feed the family.

Ken started drinking before he was thirteen. It came as naturally to him as breathing and was always there for him. He was born into a family that liked to party. By the age of fifteen, he quit school and was working full time as a carpenter to help support his family.

Ken married his first wife when he was twenty-one. A few months later, he was a new father to a baby boy. The marriage didn't last long, because his wife couldn't take the nightly parties. She left Ken. That was when he first attempted suicide.

I met him not long after that. I was a waitress, and he sat in my section. He did not leave a good first impression. I tried every trick possible to get him to leave. He finally did, but then he kept coming back, night after night.

I don't know how it happened, but soon, we were best friends, listening to each other talk about our failed relationships and offering each other support. I will never forget the night Ken told me he loved me. I told him not to say that. I didn't want to hear it. He told me he wouldn't say it unless he meant it.

One year later our daughter, Richelle, was born. Our two sons, Arin and David, followed. Over the years, things changed. Ken was drinking more and more. I have a feeling that, toward the end, there was drug use as well. Ken turned into a stranger. He had no patience with Arin's ADHD and often lashed out at him. Ken also turned on me. His greatest fear was coming true; he was becoming his father. The problem was, he refused to admit he had a problem. After all, to the rest of the world, he was happy-go-lucky Ken, the life of the party.

I tried for years to get him to get help. He didn't think he needed it. He would quit drinking for a couple of days, but he always started again. I finally made the decision to take the children and leave. I told Ken if he got help we would come back. We never got that chance. Ken drove his pickup head on into a cement pump house at eighty miles an hour. They tell me he was gone in an instant.

Someone told me not long ago that by leaving Ken, I gave him the only chance he had. I don't know about that. How could the man I loved with all my heart give up on us so easily? I will live the rest of my life with that unanswered question. I will never understand. Thank you for reading my story of survival, a story Ken ended far too soon. A story his children and I are now left to finish by ourselves.

Laura Yaklin
Ken's Wife

Kenneth Dale Jackson, Jr.
Thirty-four years old

Ken,

Today is Memorial Day. The kids and I are heading up north to the cottage for the night. Arin is excited. He's been waiting all winter to use "ol' yeller" again. He is so proud of that pole. It will always bring a smile to our faces. I can still see you standing out near the water's edge, watching that pole and just waiting, knowing for sure that at any moment a big old catfish was gonna hit.

For the first couple of years, I couldn't bear to fish alone. It just didn't seem right without you. But then I thought you'd want me to. And you'd want me to keep letting the kids do what you taught them to love.

Arin will soon be twelve. He's really struggling with your death. The emotions raging through his young mind are overwhelming at times. I pray someday he will be able to come to peace with it all. He's confused. Love and anger are an odd couple.

Richelle is such a beautiful young lady. She's fourteen now. Do you keep track of time where you are? Her hair is so long and gorgeous, just how you liked it. She's a beauty. I am having trouble handling all the boys stopping over to visit. I can just imagine your reaction.

David, your "Mr. Man," just finished his first year of school. He loved going to preschool. Your son has a thirst for knowledge that is unbelievable. His sense of humor is so much like yours. He lives for an audience, just like you did. The kids are growing up so fast. I only wish you were here with me to watch them grow.

As for me, I still think about you and miss you every day of my life. Most days, I can think of you and smile. The stabbing pain in my heart has eased to a dull ache.

I just want you to know I am doing the best I can. I am trying to raise the kids how you'd want me to. I am trying to make sure they know you loved them with all your heart. That is very important to me.

I'll never forget you, Ken. Never. I hope you are flying with the hawks and walking with the deer now. Your ashes are in the forest, where your soul can roam. I pray you are happy now. I only wish love had been enough.

Love always,

Lauri

Death Did Part Us

Lily and Harvey watched as a fire consumed their home and most of what they owned. Lily thanked God no one was hurt and that she and her husband of twenty years still had each other. Lily believed she and her family were safe. That's where she was wrong.

Lily and Harvey stood there as flames shot through the roof. They felt the heat from the wood as the temperature rose, and heard the crackle of the embers exploding in the night sky. They held hands as a lifetime of loving memories and hard work fell victim to the blaze.

Surely this would be just another low spot in a relationship that had seen its share of devastation. But it became much more when Lily found out two of Harvey's friends accidentally started the fire. It was more than Lily could take. She wanted out.

Shortly after the fire, the couple separated. Lily found a small apartment for her and the children. She then filed papers for the separation and for custody. She and Harvey had to go their own ways.

That was Harvey's breaking point. He had already faced many struggles in his life, including alcoholism, drug abuse, health problems, and the couple's miscarriage early in their marriage. Now his vision was becoming worse and he was declared legally blind. Drugs were his only comfort. Filled with self-doubt, Harvey told friends he felt like he had died in that fire.

Ironically, a North Carolina newspaper reported that someone had died in the fire. The next day the paper made a correction. Things weren't so easily fixed for Harvey.

He wanted desperately to be outdoors, to play with his children with Lily by his side. He wanted his health back so he could be free to live without pain. But instead, he felt increasingly like a burden to everyone around him.

One August morning Harvey hung himself with his own belt in a tree at a friend's house. After his death, Lily learned that was not Harvey's first suicide attempt. He had had suicidal tendencies since childhood.

None of that matters now. Lily just prays for her husband and waits for their time to be together again, a time when they can be happy. No loss, no tears, no fire. Just love.

Harvey Lee Dunn

Forty-two years old

> To My Dear Husband Harvey,
>
> Today would have been our twentieth anniversary. Where did we go astray? We were young lovers who thought it would last forever. We went through so much together—raising three children, burying one of them. So many struggles and so much pain.
>
> The fire was my breaking point. Your lifestyle of drugs and alcohol was not what I wanted our children to be around. We could have gotten back together, you know. But after nine months of our separation, you couldn't take life anymore and ended yours.
>
> Where did we go astray? I will always love you, babe; I just had to do what was best for me and our two beautiful, living children. Do you know that both are teenagers now?
>
> Soul mates, or so we thought. Death did part us. Some day I look forward to being with you again, my soul mate, best friend, and lover.
>
> Where did we go astray? I will always love ya, Harvey!
>
> Love, as always, your wife,
>
> Lily

Rhythm of My Heart

She is the song you have to play just one more time. The song you sing over and over in your mind. The one you start singing for no reason in particular. The one you never forget. I craved her energy, her passion, her very spirit. She sparked a fire in me. I can still feel that look in her eyes.

I met Stevie at a folk festival while I was vacationing in southern Texas. When I left New York City, I had no idea what to expect and certainly had no idea I would fall in love. Stevie was a beautiful young woman with razor-sharp intellect and the free spirit of a child. She could look into my soul and touch me in places I had never been touched before.

After I returned home, not a day went by that I didn't call or e-mail her. Stevie was such a breath of fresh air, and I was totally in love with her. I expressed my love for her the best way I knew how—by writing countless songs about her.

I bought her a guitar for her birthday, because she had mentioned that she would love to learn to play. Stevie really took to it and even began writing her own music. She was simply irresistible when she sang. She surprised me with a CD of her singing original songs dedicated to me. She also recorded Bob Dylan's "Blowin' in the Wind" on that same CD. No one had ever given me such a heartfelt gift.

Stevie took a leap of faith and moved to New York. She found an apartment and a job and even made plans for college. How together she seemed for such a young woman, especially since I knew she carried a lot of pain with her—the pain of sexual and physical abuse as a child. She also grew up never really having a home. Her natural mother was institutionalized several times. The abuse left scars on her heart that never quite healed. I loved her and wanted her to get help. Ironically, when she did seek help, things began to unravel.

Her introspection and bipolar diagnosis caused her to reevaluate some very basic foundations in her life. Maybe the isolation she felt from an insane childhood with a mother who had borderline personality disorder, which prevented her from fully receiving the love I offered. Maybe it was just too scary for her to be in love, with so much darkness in the background. So many maybes. No answers.

Not long after she began therapy, we sprung for a vacation in Lake Tahoe, where Stevie bought me some beautiful skis. We had an incredible time, like a couple on their honeymoon—lots of skiing, lots of making love on the snowy white mountains. It was one of the most incredible experiences I've ever had. The night before we returned to New York, she told me she was not coming home with me. She was miserably torn between her love for me and her need to be in Texas.

She went back to Texas, but was barely there one day before telling me it was a mistake. I was tired of the emotional roller-coaster, so when she moved back to New York, we started off as friends. Stevie stayed with me while she looked for a new apartment. I slept on the couch, while she slept in the bed. Our platonic relationship made her incredibly angry, and we fought all the time.

One night, after several hours of screaming, I left. But something felt strange to me, so after taking a walk, I went back home. I found her lying in my bed. She had tried to overdose on bipolar medication, about sixty ephedrine-based pills, and a bottle of wine. She left a note that said life wasn't worth living without me and that she loved me dearly.

I rushed her to the hospital. She was there for forty-five days, and no one in her family came to see her. I saw her every day, and eventually, she asked me to stop coming. She didn't realize that I still loved her dearly. So even though I knew she probably didn't mean it, I honored her request.

The night Stevie was released she came over. She was upset, and I was terrified. There at my door was the woman I loved, and the woman who tried to kill herself in my bed. I was confused and would not let her in. So we sat in the hallway and talked.

I told her to reconnect with herself, to take walks in the park, to meditate, to do some soul searching. I told her that even if she had been diagnosed with bipolar disorder, medication was only part of the solution, and she was still going to have to work through things. I told her I couldn't be there for her anymore.

I wish to God I could change those words. I wish I would have opened my arms and held her all night long. I wish I wouldn't have been so self-protective that I couldn't help someone who was so clearly crying out for help.

Two days later, she killed herself in the bathroom of a New York City hotel. I had a memorial for Stevie in Strawberry Fields, the John Lennon tribute in Central Park. Stevie loved Lennon. I drank Orangina, her favorite soft drink, played songs, lit candles, and told her spirit things I wish I would have said to her when she was still alive.

I often listen to the CD she made me. An overwhelming love for her comes over me when she sings "Blowin' in the Wind." I even used her voice on a recording of one of my songs called "Unreality." The line asks the question, "How many deaths will it take till he knows that too many people have died?"

Every time I hear her ask that, I feel as though she is speaking to me. My answer is always, "Just one, Stevie, just one."

Erik Hendin
Stevie's Boyfriend

Stephanie "Stevie" Louise Miller
Eighteen years old

"Disappear"

Sometimes I wish I was a child again
I'd play all my days away
Build my Lego blocks into something
Walk proud of that something
I know my castle would never disappear
Disappear
Sometimes I wish you weren't so innocent
And so sensitive to everything
Softest hair and deep brown eyes
Drowning there behind your smile
At some point you decided not to try
Think I'll never be the same
I have to find a way to change
I don't know how to face today
The only one who ever really knew you
You said I was the only one who understood
Damned me to hell for my whole life
To sit and think about how you died
And how I played a part in all of it
Think I'll never be the same
I have to find a way to change
Make some meaning of the mess you made
Here I'm left to clean it up

And it'll never be enough
I loved you more than you ever knew
   Forever with nothing I can do
I'll never have another chance to tell you
   To tell you
Two days before love suicide
   Bangin' on my door for help
One a.m.—I was so surprised
   I tried to protect myself
And I would never see you again
   Sometimes I wish I was a child again
I'd play all my days away
   Those days are long long gone
Now I live with this alone
   I thought my castle would never disappear
Disappear

Erik Hendin
From his CD, *Long Journey*
www.erikhendin.com

An Empty Space

Chris and Leslie became a couple the moment they laid eyes on each other. That was no easy task with Chris standing more than six feet tall and Leslie barely hitting five feet. But that's where the differences stopped and the love started.

Leslie, a single mom to two-year-old Trenton, went to an Indiana bar one cold December night to watch a football game. Chris was there to play a game of pool. Neither knew they would come face-to-face with a soul mate.

Chris opened his heart to both Trenton and Leslie, and in return, they opened their hearts to him. Soon the three became the picture of perfection, cuddled on the couch together, watching television.

Life—in love, at work, and at play—was good. Chris and Leslie talked about one day having the pitter-patter of little feet in their home. One night, as a wonderful surprise, Chris brought home Miniature Pinscher puppies named Max and Harley. The puppies made the sofa a little more crowded, but Chris said they were great practice for adding more children to their family.

Chris was passionate about the outdoors. Trenton was right there at his heels, his big blue eyes staring up at the man who showed him things he had never seen before.

Trenton now cries himself to sleep as he remembers the exciting days of watching Chris prepare for deer hunting trips, and the even more exciting days when the two would fish or search for crawdads together.

Leslie cries herself to sleep as well. She dreams of the wedding that will never take place, the vows that will never be exchanged, and the children they will never have. She knows now that Chris suffered from substance abuse. Perhaps that was his addictive personality's way of dealing with his depression. He was often able to hide those ever-increasing down days, covering his slide into an empty hole with a loving heart and a true desire to make those around him smile.

But then came those days when Chris would say to Leslie, "If anything ever happens to me . . ."

She would reply, "Nothing ever will. We are going to grow old together."

No one knew the depth of his illness until he put the gun to his head and pulled the trigger. By then it was too late. Some days Leslie doesn't have the strength to cope with Chris's death. So she just doesn't try. She doesn't get out of bed. She doesn't take a shower. She doesn't get dressed. Then she thinks of Trenton. He needs her to go on. The only way she can go on for now is with therapy, antidepressants, and sleeping pills.

An empty space lives in her soul where Chris once was. There is also his space on the sofa, a space no one can ever fill. So now mother and son hold each other. They remember what was, wish for what might have been, and wonder what will become of them.

Christopher John Bische
Twenty-four years old

My Dearest Christopher,

While I will never understand what happened to you on that fateful night, I am angry no more. But I want you to know, you never made me angrier than you did that night. The numbness and sadness sunk in hard. I cried for days, thinking of you and our time together. I never thought I would be attending your funeral only five days before your twenty-fifth birthday.

I had four wonderful years with you—loving, sharing, bonding, living. I am forever grateful to you and to God for those years. I struggle every day, wondering, did I do all that I could to help? Did I miss something? Was I not loving and caring enough? Did you love me? Did I make you sad or mad that day? Did I say something wrong? Did I do something wrong?

Your death has taught me things I wish I would not have learned this way. I learned that I love you with every piece of my heart—my entire being, my entire soul. I learned that I will love you forever and always. I learned that you were not yourself that night—that you suffered for so long, fighting the demons that had taken control. I learned that you did not do this to hurt anyone; you did it to find peace for yourself, to release yourself from the excruciating pain. I learned that this life is going to be hard without you.

Christmas Day was the one-month anniversary of your death. Except for the night you died, that was the worst day ever. What I missed most was sitting by your side watching Trenton open his gifts from Santa. I know you were watching, but it wasn't the same.

The two-month anniversary of your death was Trenton's seventh birthday. I was trying to be strong for him. Did he notice how sad I was that day? Trenton and I visited the cemetery. He brought you a balloon from his birthday party, a burgundy candle, and a stuffed monkey holding a heart. He also wrote you a letter and left it there for you to read. Your mom put the letter in your memory box.

Writing this letter is one of the hardest things I have ever done. Trying to explain my feelings and emotions is not easy, because they change so much from day to day, sometimes minute to minute.

The other night, huge thunderstorms rolled through the city. I put on my headphones and set out for a walk. It was windy, raining, and hailing. I thought about walking into the path of an oncoming car. I hoped for a tornado to carry me away into another world—the world where you are. But that didn't happen. Now I sit here, missing you so desperately, and I can't get to where you are. Do I want to? Yes. Can I? No. Am I a coward? Maybe so. But you were definitely not.

I believe we will be reunited once again, when my time on earth is done. But I can't come now. God has plans for me—things I have to finish here first. Please wait for me, Christopher. I love you, forever and always, more than you could possibly imagine.

Leslie

A Wife's Walk

Don's dry sense of humor and sensitive heart attracted Karen to the traveling salesman. Of course, the fact the he was tall, dark, and handsome didn't hurt. They were married in a small ceremony in Karen's neighborhood church where she walked down the aisle in a cathedral-length white satin gown, a veil covering the blushing brunette's cherub face.

Don stood proudly at the altar, his tuxedoed groomsmen on one side, Karen's bridesmaids in red and green velvet on the other. Their friends and family showered them with gifts to start their life together—a toaster, coffee pot, dishes, and towels. All things a young couple so desperately needs.

Karen tried to be the perfect homemaker, taking care of her husband and her home. After burning more than one pot roast, she eventually learned to make delicious dinners and had them ready when Don got home from work.

Three years after they were married, Karen became pregnant with their daughter, Rebekah. She and Don were overjoyed. This was the start of their family, and Don jumped right into the daddy role. He changed diapers, got up for middle-of-the-night feedings, and bathed his little beauty in the kitchen sink.

Karen was diagnosed with cervical cancer after Becky was born, so when baby boy Ben was added to the family, it was nothing short of a miracle. Karen and Don were devoted to their children, and they still behaved like newlyweds very much in love.

Don lived each day to its fullest and had a contagious excitement that kept his family close. Together they cheered for the first day of baseball at Fenway Park, picnicked while listening to great jazz in the Commons, and rode in a horse-drawn carriage through downtown Boston.

Don and Ben were exceptionally close. They took weekend fly-fishing trips and had contests to see who could bring home the biggest fish. Ben usually won, something that made his father very proud. That proud father was later heartbroken when his only son took his life at the age of sixteen.

Don and Karen were completely blindsided. They had only questions and no answers. Ben's death slowly took Don's life. He didn't know how to grieve for his son. Don's mother died when he was just a boy. Instead of finding comfort from his father, Don was sent to live with relatives so he could "get over it." He never grieved for her; now he had to grieve for two lost souls.

Karen and Don tried to heal from Ben's suicide by journaling their emotions. This is one of the last journal entries Don made to his son.

> I guess you just didn't know the pleasure I got from just having you around, just looking at your face, just having you with me. Simple things—stopping for coffee, a ride to a friend's house, a fishing trip, supper-table conversation. You didn't know. I told you more than once how I felt about you, how proud I was of you, but you didn't know. I guess you thought that's just how fathers talk. It's not how my father talked. You just didn't know what a world without you would be like. I know.

Don had been so strong his entire life, and he just couldn't be strong any longer. He ended his life a year and a half after his son suicided. Through it all, Karen never once doubted her husband's love for her or Becky. She knew as she walked down that church aisle that his devotion was everlasting. Her devotion to him still is.

Donald Atwood Kimball
Sixty years old

Dear Don,

I need to write to you in an effort to sort things out. I haven't been able to write to Ben as much since your death. All I seem to write are facts, not about my thoughts or feelings as I did before, which seemed to help so much.

Your death and the events immediately following it so closely paralleled Ben's death that it was like a replay, and I couldn't separate the two. They blended together, and it apparently affected my reactions.

I do remember, though, feeling angry with you for not killing me, too. I had also been seriously considering suicide and felt that you had now taken that option away from me. Then I felt angry with Ben (really for the first time) because of what he'd started. I also remember thinking that I couldn't go through this again.

It seems that I shut down mentally, physically, and emotionally. I have been living pretty much for the immediate present, seeing no future and not able to remember the past. I couldn't even feel or think about Ben's death, never mind yours. When a friend from church was killed in an accident, it unleashed all the feelings I had apparently blocked out, but my thinking is still all jumbled up.

I knew how hard Ben's death hit you, and nothing seemed to help you deal with it. I only realized how badly you were hurting when I read your writings when the police finally returned them. Then I finally understood.

So many people said that a part of you died when Ben died and that they were shocked but not surprised. I was both. I never would have believed you could end your own life. That was something I never could have imagined.

I hope you and Ben have now found your peace and that you are together again, fishing and having long discussions. Perhaps you are now getting the answers to all those "whys" that consumed our thinking for so long.

Love and peace,

Karen

You can find Karen's letter to her son Ben in "Parents Left Behind."

Pillow Feathers

"I don't know how to tell you this . . ."

With those few words, my entire life changed. I woke up to the ring of the telephone. I leaned over to answer it, thinking I would hear my boyfriend's voice. I couldn't have been more wrong. It was Brett's boss. As soon as I heard the tone in his voice, a chill ran up my spine.

"I found Brett in his garage this morning."

I jumped out of bed and began pacing with the portable phone still in my hand. I had so many questions but none would come out. So I said I would call him back, and I hung up. I walked back and forth, up and down my hallway at least a hundred times, while I tried to make sense out of that phone call.

How could Brett be dead? Surely there was a mistake. He couldn't be gone. I wasn't awake yet. I was still asleep. Maybe he was just hurt. Brett and I had spoken about eight hours before. What had we talked about? I couldn't breathe. I couldn't think. Then I fell to the floor.

Brett and I had been together for more than ten years. Like most couples, we saw our share of romantic and rocky days. But we were always there for one another, to fight the battles, to dry the tears, to kiss away the hurt. Now my best friend was gone, and the last words I said to him were, "I never want to talk to you again."

So many memories flooded my mind as I lay on the hallway floor, still holding on to the phone. It was like watching previews for a movie you've already seen. That Fourth of July in Houston when our eyes first met. His proposal at the Statue of Liberty. The Halloween we dressed up as Ninja Turtles. Our first tiny apartment in Washington state. Our first cat. Our second cat. Our move to Hawaii.

That's where he was the happiest. My mind flashed to him water skiing in Hanalei Bay, riding his bike around Diamond Head, boogie boarding at Sandy Beach. Then my mind stopped on one particular memory. Just five years to the day before I sat there crying in that tiny apartment in Green Bay, Wisconsin, I was crying for a different reason. That's when I heard the other words that changed my life.

"And the winner is . . ."

I was crowned Miss Hawaii USA. So many little girls dream about a night like that, and I was actually seeing my dream come true. I looked out at the faces in the crowd, and only one stood out. Brett. The man who encouraged me, supported me, and loved me unconditionally. He was the one who convinced me to compete for the crown. He was the one who had all the faith.

How could we have been so happy then and so desperate now? It didn't make any sense. We were very much in love, but we had a fight the night before Brett took his life. I am ashamed to admit it, but we often fought like that.

Brett's mother once told me, "Words are like feathers in a pillow. Let them out, and you will never be able to get all the feathers back in again." I never knew how right she was, until then.

I can't take back the words I said to Brett, but I can share his story to help others. Brett's life and death are part of an interactive CD-ROM being distributed by Teen Contact Crisis Line to educate teens about suicide awareness. That would make him happy. While he was with us, he spent countless hours volunteering; he fed the homeless at the Peanut Butter Ministry in Honolulu, collected toys for Toys for Tots, and was an airport greeter for the Make-a-Wish Foundation. Brett would be proud that he is still making a difference.

I will never forget those October days that changed my life. I will also never forget the words I heard from Brett every day for more than ten years. Those are the words that truly changed my life.

"I love you."

And I love him, too.

Heather Hays
Brett's fiancé

Brett Karl Herman
Thirty-eight years old

This is the letter that inspired me to write this book.

Dear Brett,

I am sitting on a hotel balcony looking out at the beautiful blue ocean that we swam in together so many times. It's weird to be here without you. And it's weird to be writing you this letter. You should be here with me. I'm mad that you're not, but I guess at least I have the memories of the fun times we had here.

I sprinkled your ashes off Waikiki a couple of days ago, and the strangest thing happened. Kevin took us out on his catamaran, and as I spread your ashes, a group of dolphins started doing corkscrews out of the water off the bow of the boat, just like they did that time we went to Kauai.

Carolyn and GeriAnn think it's a sign that you were there with us. Being on the boat surrounded by our friends, sharing stories about you, made me smile. Anyway, I just wanted you to know I was thinking about you today.

I love you always,

Heather

This is the letter I wrote after finishing this book.

Dear Brett,

It is a rainy August afternoon in Dallas. The skies are gray, and the world is wet. It's so different from the last time I wrote you a letter in Hawaii.

There is so much I want to say to you, and I just don't know where to start. I miss you so very much. I still get angry with you. Not like I used to, though. I don't scream at the air anymore. I saved the tape from the answering machine that has the last message you left for me. You told the kitties to take care of me. You told them how much you loved them and loved me. I am so thankful I didn't erase the messages that night. The kitties are with you now in heaven.

I cannot begin to explain the pain I have been through since you died. Your family was so angry with me. I didn't go to the memorial they had for you. I know they didn't understand why I didn't go. We weren't close to them and hadn't lived in Seattle in years. I was a stranger and wanted to say good-bye to you with our friends—the ones who knew you and loved you as a strong man. So I had my own memorial for you in Hawaii.

Your family and I don't speak anymore. They blame me, you know. I suppose I can't blame them, but I do hope they know that you and I loved each other very much. I still have the ring you wore on your wedding finger. Your sister thinks you threw it away. You were wearing it at the funeral home. Now it sits in my jewelry box right next to the diamond ring you gave me.

Writing this book has been cathartic for me. But I must admit, it took a toll on my relationship with Wade. I paid more attention to you in your death than I did to him, and he was right there beside me all the years I worked on this book. I loved him, and it hurt me to not be with him, but I needed to have closure with you. And the book is how I came to terms with things.

I feel sorry for all of us—for me, for you, and for those who loved and lost you. You meant so much to so many people. You know that now. I guess you didn't then. Why couldn't you have loved yourself enough to stay with us? I could ask a million questions and never get any answers. I will have my answers one day. Until then, I have my memories.

I love you, and I miss you. You were my best friend. Keep an eye on me, okay? I need that.

Forever,

Heather

Help to Heal a Love's Heart

Life is fragile. We live a tenuous existence on this fallen and frail earth. Ours is a life full of tragedy, pain, and hardship. If you are reading these words right now, you are already aware of that reality, because you are facing the tragic loss of a loved one.

But the loss you are facing is especially hard to bear because it seems so senseless, such a waste. One of the people you care deeply about took his or her own life. In all likelihood, that person woke up on the morning of the death with the expectation that this would be his or her last day on this earth. The loved one anticipated and planned the death, and that awful reality is hard for you to comprehend. You may be angry. You may have feelings of guilt. You may still be numb, afraid to unlock the feelings you have inside. But I suspect the hardest part of this experience is that you wonder why it happened. Why did something so tragic, so painful, have to take place?

When bad things happen, we ask the difficult question, "Why?" Too often, we try to answer that question with human reasoning. But usually our finite minds fail us, and we must accept the reality that we don't know all of the "whys" in life. The reassuring news, though, is that someone does know. God.

One of the greatest consolations during a time of crisis is the understanding that God has a greater purpose for our earthly suffering. That may sound trite and not what you want to hear right now, but our pain does have purpose. God does not promise an exemption from pain and suffering in this life. Suffering is inevitable. But, even when it seems to make no sense to us, God can turn it around and use it for good.

You may be a lot like me, though, when you come face-to-face with a difficult situation in life. I am like the kid in the back of the classroom with his hand up, frantically waving it for attention. "Oh, God, choose me! I don't understand. You are going too fast, God. Please, choose to answer my questions!" On the other hand, if I understand that there is a purpose behind a problem, I can trust that God is allowing certain things to happen for his greater purpose. I don't have to have all my questions answered. I can relax and know that God is in control.

By faith, we can understand and know the purpose behind suffering. The Bible says, "And we know that God causes everything to work together for the good of those who love God and are called according to His purpose for them" (Rom. 8:28, NLT). God is working in the midst of everything that happens, both good and bad. Does that mean divorce? Yes. Does that mean a financial setback? Yes. Does that mean the loss of a job? Yes. Does that even mean suicide and death? The answer is still a resounding *yes.* He uses all things, good and bad, for a greater purpose. He does not intentionally cause bad things to happen to us, but He is able to use the problems of this fallen world for our growth.

A lot of people blame God for things that He shouldn't be blamed for. But bad things happen, not because God chooses them to, but because of choices we have made. God created us with the freedom to choose right or wrong. And from the very beginning, humankind has most often chosen to do wrong. The negative experiences or losses that we face in life are due to the fact that we live in a fallen world marked by sin. The cumulative effect of the wrong choices humans have made since the dawn of time has led to the pain we experience every day.

But we love to point the finger of blame at God when things go

234

wrong in our lives, especially when we experience an unexpected loss of a loved one. God, though, is not responsible for the bad things that happen in our lives.

God could easily erase all sin and suffering at the snap of His fingers. In the blink of an eye, it could be gone. But there is only one way that He could do that. He would have to take away our freedom to choose. If we were unable to choose to go against God's will, there would be no sin, and consequently no suffering. But there would also be no real love, because the essence of love is freedom. Thankfully, God did not make us as robots but as humans with the capacity to choose Him or reject Him. He did that because He loves us and desires that we be able to love Him back of our own free will.

As creatures with a free will, we all have an ultimate choice to make regarding our relationship with God. And tragedy has a way of bringing us back to the reality of that choice. The tragedy you now face should be a wake-up call to get serious about understanding the implications of walking with God in this one and only life. It's a wake-up call for you to capture those opportunities to get answers to those deep questions of the soul.

If you have been testing the waters of faith, it's time to make a decision. Eternity may be closer than you think. You may have been drawn to church in recent days because you have this hole in your heart that you can't explain. You can't seem to get rid of the nagging fears in your life, and you are searching desperately for peace and contentment.

You may have questions and doubts about your eternal destiny. And, despite your efforts to make sense of it all, you have not been able to find the meaning of life. Tragic events have a way of knocking us down on one knee, emotionally, relationally, or in some other realm. I think God would say, "Put the other knee down and give me your life and your worship."

And I would ask you to put the other knee down and pray, "God, have your way in my life."

One day we will stand before God, and everything in our lives that has not been built on Jesus Christ and His church will crumble. Now, please understand me here; I'm not saying that God caused your loved one to take his or her own life to give you a wake-up call. It is God's prerogative to do what He will, and I do not presume to know His divine will in these matters. But I do know that God uses catalyzing events like this to bring people to Him, to remind them of important realities in life.

Jesus talked about one of these realities in His most famous sermon, the Sermon on the Mount:

> Therefore everyone who hears these words of mine and puts them into practice is like a wise man who built his house on the rock. The rain came down, the streams rose, and the winds blew and beat against that house; yet it did not fall, because it had its foundation on the rock. But everyone who hears these words of mine and does not put them into practice is like a foolish man who built his house on sand. The rain came down, the streams rose, and the winds blew and beat against that house, and it fell with a great crash. (Matt. 7:24-27)

Christ is talking about an eternal foundation here. He is contrasting those who are authentic followers of Him with those who are not. Those who obey His teaching are like the wise man who builds on rock, and those who do not obey Him are like the foolish man who builds on sand.

Many today are building their lives on treacherous foundations. Their lives are characterized by inner fears, and rightly so, because they are one storm away from disaster. Oh, they have the trappings of religion, but there is no real fruit to indicate any evidence of an authentic relationship with Jesus Christ. Their lives are built instead on power, on wealth or status, or on beliefs and philosophies that have no basis in God's eternal truth.

Many Americans today face the same choices that Solomon of old faced. Solomon, the grandest of Israel's kings, took a free fall into a forty-year abyss of partying. This sovereign was wealthier than we could ever imagine, and he used his great wealth and power to try everything "under the sun." He had seven hundred concubines at his beck and call. He sampled the finest wines and the best foods. He built expansive buildings inlayed with the purest gold and the rarest jewels. You name it, he did it.

Near the end of his life, here is what Solomon said, because he tried to do all of these things by himself, away from God, "Yet when I surveyed all that my hands had done and what I had toiled to achieve, everything was meaningless, a chasing after the wind; nothing was gained under the sun" (Ecc. 2:11).

The Bible also says, "For we brought nothing into the world, and we can take nothing out of it" (1 Tim. 6:7). All of our achievements and acquisitions become meaningless when weighed on the scales of eternity. And often it takes an event of awful proportions to bring us to our senses. Through a crisis of fear, we turn to the things that really matter in life. In the blink of an eye, many realize how fragile life is and wake up to a spiritual reality they have worked hard to ignore.

Don't ignore death or the frailty of your existence. Place your eternity in the hands of God, so that you can begin at long last to really live. Are you ready to really live? Ironically, true life is found in Christ's death. The sinless Son of God was spit upon, tortured, and hung from a cross to die for our sins. God took that evil act and made it into something wonderful for the salvation of the world, because three days later, Christ rose from the dead.

Through His death and resurrection, He conquered sin and death so that we could live forever. If you believe that—if you accept God's gift of life through the sacrifice of His Son—you will find the life you've been longing for. We have been pardoned. Our sins have been forgiven through the death, burial, and resurrection of Jesus Christ.

When we have that personal connection with Christ, the trials, the evil things, the bad circumstances—even the suicide of a loved one—all fulfill a greater purpose, because we are "called according to His purpose." While we suffer for a little while from our loss here on earth, we long for the plans and purposes of God to be fulfilled. Our suffering loosens the grip the world has on our lives, because it gives us a longing for heaven. It gives us a hope for what is to come.

If you have placed your life in the hands of God, you will find ultimate fulfillment with God in eternity. All that you have experienced, good and bad, will come together in a beautiful tapestry. You will finally be able to see what God sees as He looks down from heaven on the fabric of your life. So place your faith in God, and experience the hope that your suffering is not in vain.

Ed Young,[1]
Senior Pastor, Fellowship Church, Dallas/Fort Worth, TX
www.fellowshipchurch.com

---

1. Ed Young is the founding and senior pastor of Fellowship Church. Known for its creativity and innovation, the church is now one of the ten largest in the country. The author of more than half a dozen books, Pastor Young received his Master of Divinity from Southwestern Baptist Theological Seminary. He and his wife Lisa have been married twenty years and have four children.

Why Writing Heals

"Choose Life"

Yes, there is life after death
  Man is a spirit
When the spirit separates from the body
  The body dies
The spirit either goes to heaven or hell
  The choice is up to us
We can choose either eternal life or destruction
  Choose life

—Robby Wirick
  Suicided at twenty-seven years old

The Power of the Pen

Change is part of life. Just as spring blooms and summer is followed by fall and winter, a time of recovery and rejuvenation, change is part of living.

Loss is a part of our movement through life; without it, no renewal can occur. However, no one is well-equipped to deal with the loss of a loved one. No matter how much thought we put into it, or how much the death is anticipated, we are in new territory when it happens. We are even less able to deal with an unexpected loss, particularly the suicide of a person we love.

One way of dealing with any emotional event is to gather our thoughts and reflect upon them. We can then begin to understand what we are experiencing. Writing provides us with a tool to do exactly that—to make sense of what we see as a senseless act, to understand our roles in that act, and to know what roles we have to play in the future.

We don't do this to get these emotions behind us, to simply "get on with life." We do it to gain perspective on the relationships with our loved ones, to see how the loss has made us different, and to learn how we can incorporate that into the rest of our lives.

Writing is one of the most powerful tools that humankind has developed. It allows us to capture our thoughts and feelings at a particular moment—those that cause us joy or sadness, sorrow or glee, desperation or fulfillment. Memory is short, fallible, and fading, yet we still need to capture those moments that are important to us.

Just as we take photographs to help us recall vacations or family re-unions, some people chronicle the events of their days in journals. Our lives can be so much more rounded and complete if we write about what we experience and reflect as we write. Journaling helps us understand the nature of our days and our emotions.

The passage of time makes us different people. What we experience now is going to be different when we recall it later. Only if we write about our actions now, will we be able to recapture our thoughts and feelings with any accuracy.

Writing allows us to reflect on the interactions we have with others, to give life to those emotions that we may have felt at some level but which remained unexpressed. We can give life to those memories by reading later what we have written. We cannot know when we lose someone what the effects of that loss will be until much time has passed. Journaling chronicles those effects.

Writing can help us make our heroes and our demons ours to control, and make us realize we are the masters. We can become the victor over any adversity. We write to help process the events in our lives, and ultimately feel freer from them. Productive or destructive, all our relationships are part of us, forever. How we choose to make those relationships work for us in our future is up to us.

Writing can help us be in charge of those encounters and of the inevitable change. Change will come and go like the seasons come and go. But understanding the change and reflecting on it allows us to move from winter to spring and from summer to fall.

Dr. J. Ray Hays, JD, PhD[1]

---

1. Dr. J. Ray Hays currently serves as an independent consultant on legal cases revolving around mental health issues. He served as a professor in the Department of Psychiatry and Behavioral Sciences at the University of Texas-Houston Medical School for more than twenty years. He has edited and written dozens of nonfiction books and is a fellow of the American Association of State Psychology Boards, as well as a member of the editorial board for *Psychological Reports*.

A Letter from You
To Keep or To Share

"To My Son"

Hold on to my wings
For I know you will be the one to give them to me

— Bonnie Renicks
 Rob's mother
 Rob suicided at twenty-six years old

Dear Friend,

Please use these pages to write your own thoughts. Many of those who wrote letters for this book said it was one of the most difficult things they had ever done. But all of them found comfort when they finished.

Crisis Support

"Soundproof"

What can I do when no one hears me cry?
   What can I do when I want to die?
Why is it no one ever sees my tears
   Even though I freely express my fears?
Why do they not help me?
   Why do they not care?
Their incomprehension just isn't fair
   Listen to me
What I say is no lie
   I am unhappy, and I want to die
I could scream and scream, till I could scream no more
   But the ears of my friends are a soundproof door

— Susan Elizabeth Jones
   Suicided at fifteen years old

Warning Signs

Many of us left behind after suicide have overwhelming feelings of guilt. We think we should have seen what was going on in the life of our loved one. It is often too painful, and always fruitless, to second-guess the circumstances of suicide. But we can be aware of the warning signs that most people who suicide display, especially since the decision is rarely a spur-of-the-moment one. Here are just some of the warning signs:

- Verbal cues: "I can't go on." "Nothing matters any more."

- Writing about death or suicide.

- Changes in attitude, appearance, or behavior.

- Drug or alcohol abuse.

- Depression or isolation.

- Self-mutilation.

- Sudden weight loss or gain.

- Loss of self-worth.

- Feelings of loneliness or sadness.

- Impulsiveness.

- Fighting.

- Lack of energy.

- Disturbed sleep patterns—sleeping too much or too little.

Don't Be Left Behind

When we see someone we care about in pain, our natural instinct is to take that pain away. But sometimes we just can't. Sometimes the best thing for us to do is listen—listen without judging, listen without jumping in, and listen to our loved one's heart.

If you are feeling suicidal, the most important thing you can do is talk. Talking about feelings is difficult, especially when you feel so vulnerable, but it could save your life. Talk to anyone—family, friends, a doctor, or a crisis hotline worker. If you think someone you love is considering suicide, here are some things you can do to help:

- Give him or her your undivided attention.

- Be careful when offering advice and solutions.

- Offer a safe place to talk with no judgment.

- Don't try to take charge.

- Put the person at ease.

- Don't analyze, criticize, or categorize.

- Don't offer blanket statements like "Things will get better."

- Don't interrogate.

- Try to see things from the other person's perspective.

Hotlines

911 – In an emergency, always call 911 first.

- Toll-free nationwide in the US, 24 hours a day/7 days a week.
  1-800-LIFENET or 1-800-543-3638

- In the US or Canada, call the Covenant House Nineline anytime.
  1-800-999-9999

- If you are a child or a teen in trouble, call this hotline from Girls
  and Boys Town, anytime day or night.
  1-800-448-3000

- International Hotlines
  If you live or travel outside of the US, log onto
  www.befrienders.org for crisis hotlines in other countries.

- State Hotlines
  1-800-SUICIDE or 1-800-784-2433

For crisis hotlines in all US states, go to www.suicidehotlines.com. This Web site lists hotline phone numbers for every state, as well as support group information.

Web Sites

www.afsp.org

The American Foundation for Suicide Prevention (AFSP) site lists suicide support groups in every state, as well as research information and the latest statistics.

www.contactcrisisline.org

CONTACT is a national network of crisis intervention and telephone help line centers. Log on to find hotlines and crisis awareness. I have been on the board of directors for years, and it is an amazing organization. The volunteers are incredible.

www.erikhendin.com

Singer-songwriter Erik Hendin is a survivor of suicide, and he uses music to heal. He has performed on a national stage for the suicide awareness organizations AFSP, AAS, and SPAN. Erik composed the music for the documentary *A Secret Best Not Kept,* which you can find at www.sayitoutloud.com. You can find Erik's story in "Rhythm of My Heart.*"*

www.nami.org

The National Alliance for the Mentally Ill (NAMI) is a nonprofit, self-help organization for consumers, families, and friends of people with severe mental illnesses. The site lists local affiliates, as well as legislative and consumer news.

www.parentsofsuicide.com and **www.angelfire.com/ga4/ffos**

These sites offer online support for parents of suicides (POS) and friends and families of suicides (FFOS). Both were started by Karyl Chastain-Beal after the death of her daughter (see "Rainbows and Butterflies").

www.road2healing.com

Louise Wirick started the Survivors Road2Healing Web site after her son died. You will find self-help information, online support groups, and links to other resources (see Louise's story in "Survivors Road2Healing").

www.spanusa.org

The Suicide Prevention Action Network (SPAN) shares the newest legislation in suicide awareness and prevention. You can also find other valuable links on this page.

www.starfishfoundation.org

The Starfish Foundation started as a one-woman operation. Belita Nelson almost lost her son to a drug overdose. Now she and her son tour the country teaching others about drug abuse awareness, mental health issues, and suicide prevention. Read Belita's story in "Rocky Mountain Memory."

www.suicidology.org

The American Association of Suicidology (AAS) is a national clearinghouse for suicide awareness, research, and understanding.

Those Left Behind
How to Get in Touch

"Dan"

The white house with chipped paint sits back
    in the frosty rolling hills
Neighing horses mourn in the cool evening air
    He zips over black paved roads on his BMX
Tires purring, feet incessantly pushing pedals
    Shaggy gray dog trying to keep up
He thinks of the supper that awaits him
    And the supple warmth of the old wood stove
The early Autumn wind sweetly sweeps through his
    dirty blonde hair
Green eyes fixed steady on the road ahead
    He's late for dinner once again

—Jason
  Age ten
    Jason's brother, Danny Bossard, suicided at nineteen

E-mail Addresses

Children Left Behind

"All My Loving," The Pratt Children—ncarfan88@aol.com

"Can We Call Heaven?" The Smart Children—heather@heatherhays.com

"Changing Face of Father," Pidge Koehler—pidge97@aol.com

"Gone Fishin'," Jan Fields—daytonajan@columbus.rr.com

"Hidden Treasures," Tracy Deupree—tracyntx@cox.net

"Mr. Bear, Junior," Kelly Wells—heather@heatherhays.com

"My Grandma," Austin Reid—tracyntx@cox.net

"Never-ending Story," Linda Marquez—missingray@aol.com

"Over the Rainbow," The Bloy Children—dvanwychen@aol.com

"Remembering New Year's," Melissa Pacheco—Melissa_@pacbell.net

"Sounds of the Season," Michelle Ray—fettsray@aol.com

"Waking Up," Christine Stone-Monaghan—monaghanchristine@hotmail.com

Friends Left Behind

"A Teen's Insight," Leslie DeLuna—leslie@runningwiththewind.com

Brenda Adkins—2redsmom@runningwiththewind.com

"Dawn's Sunrise," Dawn Bennett—fourcsmom05@aol.com

"Forever Missed," Kristin Ross—kristinross7@yahoo.com

"Friends Never Leave," Kaylen Denning—kaylendenning@hotmail.com

"Little Boy Lost," Lori Shuford—dodieanne@hotmail.com

"Rocky Mountain Memory," Belita Nelson—www.starfishfoundation.org

"Soul Sisters," Tonya Pike—tlpike@charter.net

"The Music Never Ends," Maria-Felix Garza—bassie0785@yahoo.com

"The War and the Wall," Lynda Greene-Kahler—degeorgeatunionstation@juno.com

"Weaving Words," Mary Van Wychen—dvanwychen@aol.com

Loves Left Behind

"A Wife's Walk," Karen Kimball—karencck2001@yahoo.com

"An Empty Space," Leslie Duncan—leslie.duncan@bms.com

"Death Did Depart Us," Lily Dunn—lilybelldunn@charter.net

"From Malta With Love," AnnMarie Chetcuti—annmarie@waldonet.net.mt

"Goodnight Moon," Susan Bloy—dvanwychen@aol.com

"Leaving Las Vegas," Tishia Lei Ponce—pictureit02@yahoo.com

"Love's First Loss," Brandi Alexander—lanayalexander@aol.com

"Nazarene Water Truck," Linda McKee—lindamckee@hotmail.com

"Pillow Feathers," Heather Hays—www.heatherhays.com

"Rebel With a Cause," Tracy Murphy—dmurphy10@wi.rr.com

"Rhythm of My Heart," Erik Hendin—www.erikhendin.com

"Something Blue," Linda Marquez—missingray@aol.com

"Unfinished Life," Laura Yaklin—justbeingme825@aol.com

Parents Left Behind

"A River So Deep," Charlene Grimmett—chargrimm@aol.com

"Absent Without Leave," Alice Isabell—mom2randy@earthlink.net

"Chocolate Kisses," Kristi Valis—sccricket13@sc.rr.com

"Garden of Angels," Sandra Marx—sandram@elliott.co.za

"Hindsight," Marie-Clare De Vere—jollyjournalist@hotmail.com

"Homemade Heart," Carol Loehr—Rloehr8080@aol.com

"It's that Simple," Karen Kimball—karencck2001@yahoo.com

"Phoenix Rising," Willis Day—nathan12401@yahoo.com

"Rainbows and Butterflies," Karyl Chastain-Beal—arlynsmom@cs.com

"Ray of Sunshine," Linda Marquez—missingray@aol.com

"Red Roses for His Birthday," Kim Hargrove—kingsws6mom@aol.com

"Survivors Road2Healing," Louise Wirick—www.road2healing.com

"The Purple Connection," Monika Lewis—buttercup43402@yahoo.com

"Undaunted Courage," Dick Loehr—Rloehr8080@aol.com

"Wednesday's Child," Carole Riggs—hunybachlady@yahoo.com

"White Candlelight," Kathleen Kay Braden—kat5343605@yahoo.com

Siblings Left Behind

"Board Walk in the Rain," Sophie Metz—heather@heatherhays.com

"Bubba Shawn," Nick Cioffe—kat5343605@yahoo.com

"Dial M for Mistake," Vickey Thomas—vickeyb@progressivetel.com

"Hearts Made Us Friends," Shirley Brunson—heather@heatherhays.com

"Here's to You, Jude," Mark Brown—markallenbrown@earthlink.net

"How Tight They Pinch," Peggy Wagner—missdallasusa@yahoo.com

"Mona Lisa in a Silver Frame," Lya Rijkse—l.rijkse@gmx.net

"Red, White, and Bootsie," Laurel Santee—greyhoundmama@sbcglobal.net

"See You Tomorrow," Tiyana Mardesich—larfta2@aol.com

"St. Patrick's Day Blessing," Jennifer Foust—jenknee27@aol.com

"There Went My Hero," Christa Slade—www.road2healing.com

Other Contributors

Foreword

Christian@skillsenhancement.com

Help to Heal Your Heart

"Help to Heal a Child's Heart," Linda Runnells—ladyprof2001@yahoo.com

"Help to Heal a Friend's Heart," Diane Weatherford—d_weatherford@earthlink.net

"Help to Heal a Love's Heart," Pastor Ed Young—www.edyoung.org

"Help to Heal a Parent's Heart," Charlotte Dunhill—dunhill2@msn.com

"Help to Heal a Sibling's Heart," Dr. Norman Giddan—jgiddan@mco.edu

"The Power of the Pen," Dr. Ray Hays—jrayhays7@yahoo.com

Poems

"Angel of My Heart," Tena Rae—www.tenarae.net

"Blood Brothers," Wade Hendricks—wade_hendricks@hotmail.com

"Choose Life," Robby's Mother, Louise Wirick—louise@road2healing.com

"Dan," Jason and Danny's Mother, Sandy Nowalk—pnowalk@twcny.rr.com

"How Long," Wade Hendricks—wade_hendricks@hotmail.com

"Soundproof," Susan's Mother, Kristi Valis—sccricket13@sc.rr.com

"Story of My Life," Lya Rijske—l.rijkse@gmx.net

"Tell Me," Eileen Shaw—emsgss@aol.com

"To My Son," Bonnie Renicks—brenicks@teknology.net

"Who Will Walk With Me?" Kevin Johnson—kpjmusic@yahoo.com

Never Alone
A Thought Left Behind

"Story of My Life"

You are the story of my life

   You are the one who saw me through the night

You've been right here by my side

   Your love and kisses were never denied

If I wrote a book, you would be in every line

   Through all of time

You are the story of my life

—Lya Rijkse
   Yvonne Van Lieshout's sister
   Yvonne suicided at twenty-one years old

Healing Hearts

Life sometimes takes us on a path so winding, we wonder how we will ever find our way back home. After all, at the end of the day, home is exactly where we want to be—safe, warm, and protected. But when we lose someone we love, we often wonder how to go on without feeling like the walls are crashing in around us.

The answer I found in my search, and by talking to dozens of others for this book, is that we go on because we are survivors and that is what we do. We have family and friends who love and support us, and who would be devastated to lose us. We must survive for them, and for ourselves. Those of us left behind feel, at times, an almost unbearable pain, and the suffocating cloud of confusion. But life is worth living, and life does move forward. You will, at your own pace, join that movement.

My personal journey toward healing started with an overwhelming amount of pain; I felt abandoned, ashamed, and angry after my fiancé's suicide. It took a lot of tears, talking, and therapy to get through the shock and denial, but I did it. You can, too.

I find rays of hope in my family, my friends, and my faith; I use those rays to move one step further in the healing process. I also find hope in my memories. Brett and I gave each other strength. He still gives me strength when I reflect on our life together. I think back to the day we stepped off a plane at the Honolulu airport. We had never been to Hawaii before, but we knew we wanted to make it our home. It didn't matter that we had no jobs, no place to live, and very little money. We had each other, and that was enough.

A Thought Left Behind

I still don't understand why Brett left us, but after all these years, I smile a lot more when I think of him. I smile when I remember the dance he did every morning when getting ready for work. I smile when I think of how he rescued our kitty, Calvin, from a garbage bin. I smile when I read the beautiful cards he wrote to me over the years. I keep those cards tucked away for the private love story I still, from time to time, read.

Treasure your memories and share your stories—write them down, draw pictures, get your family together and talk. There are so many ways to honor your loved one, and at the same time to heal yourself. I hope you can take care of your heart and find the path to a positive life. Your pain is real, but so is life. Embrace it, knowing one day you will have all the answers you are seeking.

Each day is a chance for you to change your life. Each sunrise offers hope, if you can only open your heart to it. I know it's hard. No one said the path you are on is easy. But reach out to those close to you, and those in this book, and recognize that you are not alone. That is one thing I can promise you: you are never alone.

Thank you for reading these stories and for keeping the memories of our loved ones alive. Take care of yourself and be safe on your life's journey. You will find your way home again. You will feel safe again. Look forward to that day because if you let it, it will come.

—Heather Hays

About the Author

Heather Hays was born in Athens, Georgia, and grew up in Houston, Texas. She graduated *summa cum laude* from Chaminade University of Honolulu with a BS in behavioral sciences. Before earning a master's degree in television and film from Boston University, she was crowned Miss Hawaii USA, and she competed in the Miss USA pageant.

Heather began her career in television news more than fifteen years ago as a weathercaster and general assignment reporter, shooting and editing her own stories. Today, she is an anchor in one of the country's largest media markets. Industry recognition includes Edward R. Murrow, AP, RTNDA, and Katie awards. Heather sits on the board of directors for CONTACT, a crisis and counseling hotline, and she lives in Dallas, Texas.

You can find out more about Heather at www.heatherhays.com.